A SENSE OF LIFE

By the *Author of:* NIGHT FLIGHT

SOUTHERN MAIL

WIND, SAND AND STARS

FLIGHT TO ARRAS

AIRMAN'S ODYSSEY

THE LITTLE PRINCE

THE WISDOM OF THE SANDS

A SENSE OF LIFE

Antoine de Saint-Exupéry

A SENSE
OF LIFE

FUNK & WAGNALLS COMPANY, INC.

NEW YORK

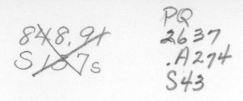
Except for the material described below, this book
has been translated from the French by Adrienne Foulke.

Grateful acknowledgment for the use in this volume of some material
from *Wind, Sand and Stars*, copyright, 1939, by Antoine de Saint-Exupéry
is made to Harcourt, Brace & World, Inc., by whose permission it is reprinted; and to the New York *Times* for "An Open Letter to Frenchmen
Everywhere," © 1942, by The New York Times Company and reprinted
by their permission.

Contents

Contents

viii

INTRODUCTION

Introduction

This collection presents the shorter writings of Saint-Exupéry, arranged chronologically. They will come as a revelation to many readers, for they offer aspects of his work that are not widely known—short fiction, foreign news correspondence, political essays, and prefaces.

The first selection is the earliest example we have of Saint-Exupéry's writing. It is an excerpt from "The Escape of Jacques Bernis," the complete text of which has been lost. Through Jean Prévost, who was on the editorial staff of *Le Navire d'Argent*, the magazine directed by Adrienne Monnier, this material appeared in the April, 1926, issue under the title "The Aviator." Prévost was impressed by the young author's gift for direct and truthful expression. Some passages do reveal a maturity that shows Saint-Exupéry was already in possession of his highly individual style.

The second major group of pieces includes the dispatches that Saint-Exupéry wrote from the Soviet Union and from Spain as special correspondent for *Paris-Soir* and *L'Intransigeant*.

In late April, 1935, he returned to Paris from a lecture tour that he had made through various Mediterranean countries together with two other fliers, Jean-Marie Conty and André Prévot. He left almost immediately for Moscow and arrived in time to witness the May Day celebrations.

On December 29 of the same year, Saint-Exupéry embarked on the ill-starred attempt to better the flying-time record from Paris to Saigon. The account of his disastrous accident over the desert became a major chapter in *Wind, Sand and Stars*. The venture left him heavily in debt, and he eagerly accepted an offer from *L'Intransigeant* to go to Spain. His dispatches from Barcelona and the Lérida front are dated August, 1936, one month after the outbreak of the Civil War.

In the early summer of 1937, he returned to Spain as special correspondent for *Paris-Soir*, writing this time from the Madrid and Carabanchel fronts.

Saint-Exupéry's reportage has its own particular and unusual interest, because here we find his impressions in their most spontaneous form and we are brought immediately to the heart of his thinking. Entire passages in his later book *Wind, Sand and Stars* were drawn from this material—for example, the "Murdered Mozart" and the "Spanish Sergeant" passages. In some instances, he used the early material integrally, in others he reworked it. Also, many characteristic preoccupations and themes—the respect for man, death, passion, justice, order, compassion—that he was to develop further in *The Wisdom of the Sands* are first formulated in his foreign dispatches.

The series of articles under the general title "Peace or War?" was written after Munich, in October, 1938, at the request of *Paris-Soir*. (Sections of this material reappeared in *Wind, Sand and Stars* in an abbreviated and recast form.) Here Saint-Exupéry reveals his deep concern for the future of France and of Europe; he searches desperately for evidence of human brotherhood in the midst of the confusion and conflict that he foresaw as the prelude to a general collapse. He incorporated in this material a recollection from his Spanish experience, when enemy voices spoke to each other in the night from their opposing hillside trenches. These same torments gripped André Malraux, who gave them expression in *Man's Hope*.

The last of these three essays—"We Must Give Meaning to Men's Lives"—is the most moving. Here we find the note that was to be sounded again in the "Letter to General X"—Saint-Exupéry's horror of war and his dismay at living in a period which turns man into a robot and robs him of even the time to think. He expressed certain ideas here—about contradictions, the shepherd, the sentinel, the peasant—that he returned to in *The Wisdom of the Sands*, which appeared posthumously.

Saint-Exupéry had been appointed manager of Aeropostal Argentina, an affiliate of the French-owned Compagnie Générale Aéropostale, in October, 1929. In this capacity, he was responsible for plotting the last and southernmost section of the company's air routes. Like his fellow pilots and friends Guillaumet and Mermoz, Saint-Exupéry flew many reconnaissance missions. It was during one of these, as he was flying over Patagonia, that he ran into the cyclone of which he wrote in "The Pilot and the Elements." Later reproduced in *Wind, Sand and Stars* as "The Elements," this famous piece appeared originally in the August, 1939, issue of the weekly *Marianne*. It has often been compared to Conrad's *Typhoon*. Indeed, Saint-Exupéry makes an explicit reference to Conrad: he speaks of a man's inability to communicate the exact meaning of a dramatic experience. He cannot grasp it at the moment of living it because of the very violence of the action; when he re-creates the experience in memory, the horror he evokes is "something invented after the fact."

"An Open Letter to Frenchmen Everywhere" was written hurriedly after the Allied landings in North Africa, which were followed by the Germans' moving into the southern zone of France. It called upon all Frenchmen to unite. The appeal was broadcast over all the French-language short-wave facilities of the Office of War Information, published in North African papers and in *Le Canada* of Montreal; in English, it appeared in the *New York Times Magazine*. It inspired the last chapter of *"Lettre à un Hostage"* and also makes one think of the concluding lines of *Flight to Arras:* "The defeated have no right to speak. No more right to speak than has the seed."

"Letter to General X" was written in July, 1943, at the North African air base where Saint-Exupéry was stationed. As in "Peace or War?" again he gives passionate expression to the urgency of infusing men's lives with spiritual meaning.

In 1933 and in 1938, Saint-Exupéry wrote two prefaces to major books on flying—one of them Anne Lindbergh's *Listen! the Wind*—and the introduction to a special issue of *Document* dedicated to test pilots. Even when he is writing a preface, Saint-Exupéry leads us to the heart of the matter: "What is essential? Maybe it is not the exhilaration or the strain or the danger but the point of view to which these things lift us."

In this book, we discover Saint-Exupéry carrying out specific assignments or responding to specific situations, and writing in forms that are not his habitual modes of expression. It is heartening to enter so quickly into direct contact with the point of view of a man of action and reflection who wishes to give meaning to men's lives.

—Claude Reynal

A SENSE OF LIFE

I.

THE AVIATOR

The following pages are from an early novella by Saint-Exupéry, "L'Évasion de Jacques Bernis." The complete manuscript has been lost, and we have only the excerpts selected by Jean Prévost and published in *Le Navire d'Argent*, April, 1926. Prévost was killed in the Vercors, the mountain range that served as a natural fortress for the French Resistance, in July, 1944, one day after Saint-Exupéry disappeared over France while on an Allied reconnaissance flight.

Prévost had added these comments to the excerpted "The Aviator": "Saint-Exupéry is a specialist in aviation and mechanical engineering. I met him at the home of friends and greatly admired his vigor and finesse in describing his impressions as a pilot. When I learned that he had actually put them in writing, I was very eager to read them. He had lost his first version, I believe, had rewritten it from memory (he composes everything in his head before putting it down on paper), and worked it into a story, excerpts of which appear here. He has a gift for directness and truth that seems to me amazing in a beginning writer. I believe Saint-Exupéry is at work on other stories."

The powerful wheels strain against the chocks.

As far as fifty feet behind the plane, the grass is flattened by the propeller blast and it flows like water. One turn of the pilot's wrist unleashes or stills this storm.

He guns the engine and the roar swells until sound becomes a dense, almost solid ambience enclosing his body. When he senses that the roar has climaxed, he says with a sense of satisfaction "Good." And with the back of his fingers he brushes the longerons: no vibration. This condensed energy rejoices his heart.

He leans out of the cockpit: "So long! . . ." The figures on the ground who have come for this dawn farewell are garbed in long trailing shadows. But the pilot, on the threshold of a three-thousand-mile leap through the sky, is already far removed from them. He glances at the nose of his plane outlined against the light; it is a black short-snouted cannon leaning on the sky. Beyond the propeller, the landscape shimmers in mist.

The engine is idling now. Final handclasps are released quickly, like the casting off of the ropes. In an eerie silence, he buckles his seat belt, two parachute straps, and then, with a settling movement of his shoulders and torso, fits the cockpit

5

to his body. This is it . . . takeoff. From now on, he belongs to another world.

One last glance at the instrument panel, a horizon of dials narrow but expressive—the altimeter is carefully set at zero. One last glance at the thick, stubby wings. A wave—"Okay!" —and he is free.

Rolling slowly into the wind, he pushes the throttle forward. The engine kindles in a series of quick explosions, and snatched up by the propeller, the plane thrusts ahead. The bucking soon abates. The pilot, gauging his speed by the action of his control sticks, communicating his will through them, feels his dominion over this new world take hold and expand.

Below him, the elastic ground slips by like a conveyor belt. The air, impalpable when first tested, becomes fluid, then solid, and leaning against it, the pilot climbs upward.

The hangars that flank the runway, the trees, the hills, deliver up the horizon to him in turn, and in turn disappear. At six hundred feet, he is still leaning out over a toy landscape with tiny upright trees and painted houses; the forest is still a thick fur. Then the earth is swept bare.

The air is rough now, flowing in short, hard waves, and the plane stumbles and rears against them. Gusts of wind slap the wings, and the whole plane reverberates. But, as a fulcrum steadies a pendulum, the pilot holds it to its course.

At nine thousand feet he reaches stillness. The sun is caught fast in the rigging; now there are no swirling currents to dislodge it. Far below, the earth has frozen into immobility.

6

The pilot adjusts the ailerons, the stabilizer, and, heading for Paris, calculates his drift. Then, preparing to slip for ten hours into somnolence, he moves only through time. . . .

The motionless waves unfurl a vast fan over the surface of the sea.

The sun has at last twinned the far strut to its shadow.

A sense of physical unease has roused the pilot. He checks. Tachometer needle steady. He looks down: sea. Then a noisy cough from the engine darkens his consciousness like a fainting spell. Instinctively, he advances the throttle. It is nothing—a drop of water in the fuel line. Gently he cuts the engine back to a conforting steady hum. A cold sweat . . . h'm, he would not have thought he'd have been afraid.

Gradually he rediscovers the particular slope of the back, the exact support for the elbow required for his peaceful well-being.

The sun now hangs overhead. Fatigue feels good to him so long as he need not stir, so long as he nowhere jostles this torpor that enfolds him, so long as the gentlest pressure on the controls will suffice.

The oil pressure drops, then rises. What's going on in there?

The engine shivers. Bastard! The sun has wheeled to the left; it is already turning red.

A clanking protest in the engine. . . . A connecting rod? No. . . . Distributor?

7

The nut on the throttle has worked loose and he must steady it by hand. Blasted thing!

It could be a connecting rod, at that.

This is how one notices—from shortness of breath, waggling teeth, gray hair—that the whole body has grown suddenly old.

So long as it holds out until he reaches the field. . . .

The earth is reassuring. The pilot drops lower to savor its neatly carved fields, its geometric forests, its villages. From on high the earth looked naked and dead. As the plane sinks lower, the earth is clothed again. It is once more tufted with trees; it swells with the rise and fall of hills and valleys; it breathes. The mountain he is flying over is the chest of a reclining giant that expands until it almost touches him. He aims the nose of his plane toward a garden that spreads wide its tree clumps and opens before him on a human scale.

"Engine's humming along now!" Then what about those noises he heard? He no longer believes in them. Yet so close to the earth, they are a matter of life and death.

He hugs the curving plains, slips between rolling hilltops like a length of cloth passing through the rollers of a press, draws the fields up to him and casts them behind, tempts the poplars with the quick, flashing strokes of a racket, feints, and sometimes swoops up and away from the earth like a fighter catching his breath.

Now he scuds in toward the airport, skimming over the roofs of windowed factories (light here), ruffling the leafy crowns of city parks (dark here). And springing from an inexhaustible horizon, the torrential earth sweeps under him, a flood of roofs, walls, trees.

The landing is a letdown. The river of wind, the rumble of the engine, and the final gravelly turn on the runway—all this he exchanges for a suffocating, silent world—a poster landscape of dead-white hangars, green carpets, neatly trimmed poplars, and young Englishwomen, with tennis rackets under their arms, stepping down from the blue Paris-London planes.

He lets his body slip down in the sticky cockpit. Figures rush toward him. "Capital! Capital!" . . . Officers, friends, star-gazers. . . . Weariness grips his shoulders suddenly. "We'll lift you out!" He lowers his head and stares at his hands, glistening with oil. He feels sobered, despondent, weary unto death.

Now he is plain Jacques Bernis, wearing a jacket that smells of camphor. He moves around the room inside a clumsy, numb body. He glances absently at the luggage arranged neatly, too neatly, in the corner, bespeaking how everything here is unsettled and temporary. This room has still to be taken possession of by books, by clothing.

"Hello. . . . Is that you?" He ticks off the amenities, accepts the exclamations, the congratulations.

"Back from the dead! Good for you!" . . .

"Of course, of course." . . .

"And when will I see you?" . . .

"Not free today, as it happens." . . .

"Tomorrow?" . . .

"Tomorrow—let me see." . . .

"Golf tomorrow, but come along." . . .

"Not interested?" . . .

"Well, then, day after tomorrow—dinner—eight sharp."

Bernis walks along the street. He feels as if he is striding upstream against the current of this crowd. As if he is personally meeting every single face in this human river. Now and then a face touches him to the quick; it is a vision of peace. Take this woman, and life would be peace, all peace. . . . Some of the men's faces are craven, and then Bernis feels strong.

He wanders into a dance hall, and without taking off his padded explorer's coat, shoulders his burly way through a crowd of gigolos. They live their night life in this amusement tank like so many goldfish in a bowl, floating from a song to a dance to a drink and back again. In this dim, shelving world where he alone has his wits about him, he feels like a fumbling, overladen porter. His mind is lusterless. He walks stiffly among the tables toward a free place at the bar. Women's eyes meet his, glance away, and to him they seem to turn opaque. Young people nimbly retreat to let him pass. He remembers making his night rounds, and how the cigarettes drop from the sentinels' fingers as he draws near.

He is assigned to the pilot-training program and today is lunching in the only restaurant near the field. At the next table, some noncommissioned officers are finishing their coffee. Bernis listens. "They do a real job. I love these fellows." They are discussing the runway ("too muddy") and the bonus pay for convoy duty, and, finally, the day's adventure. "There I was, at three hundred feet and with water in the transmission. Some fix! Not a landing field anywhere within miles, just a farmyard a little way back. What the hell! I ease down, trim the plane, and bounce along right into the manure pile." They all laugh. "Like the time I ended up in a haystack," the adjutant reminisced. "I turn around to see where my passenger is—a lieutenant, wouldn't you know! Gone. Vanished. I found him sitting on the other side of the hayrick."

Some men don't walk away alive from a thing like that, Bernis reflects, but for these fellows it's all in a day's work. I like the way they talk about it. Like an official report, terse. I like these men. I'm not strong on group spirit, but with fellows like these you can be simple.

"Do tell me what it's like. How it feels." That's what women ask you.

"Pichon? Student?"
"Yes."
"Ever flown before?"
"No."
Well, at least he won't be full of a lot of preconceived ideas. It's the student-observers who think they know it all. They've memorized all the rules, haven't they? "Stick to the left. . . . Now the right foot. . . ." Not easy students.

"I'll take you up. First time round, you just watch." They climb in.

The mechanic is working for the school on contract. He gives a languid flick to the propeller. He has six months and eight days of turning propellers to look forward to. This morning he even scratched it on the wall of the W.C.: as he figured it, that made about ten thousand propeller turns. Day in, day out. So. . . .

The student looks at the sky, which is blue, at some treelike shapes—ah! it's a herd of cows browsing along the runway. His instructor is polishing the throttle with his sleeve; it feels good to see it shine. The mechanic is counting the turns—up to twenty-two already. What a way to earn a living! "Suppose you clean the sparkplugs once in a while!" There, that'll give him something to think about.

An engine starts—well, an engine starts when it is good and ready to start. Better leave it alone. . . . Thirty, thirty-one, and it catches.

Danger, heroism, air intoxication. What do these words mean? The student no longer understands them.

The plane is airborne before the student realizes he has left the ground, but now he can see the hangars below him. Wind massages his cheeks; he stares at the instructor's back.

Good God! What's happening? They're losing altitude. The earth streams by to right and left. He holds on grimly. The ground? Where is it? He sees only a clump of trees revolving slowly, pushing up, up, then a railway track suspended vertically, then the sky . . . and suddenly the airfield stretches flat and smooth before them, just below the wheels. The student feels them touch the ground, the wind falls, and they're down. . . . The man turns around and laughs, and the student struggles to take it all in.

"Basics," Bernis explains. "The moment something abnormal happens, you cut your engine. Point one. Point two, take off your goggles. Point three, hold on for dear life. You loosen your belt only in case of fire. Clear?" Clear.

Here at last were the words the student had been waiting for. Words that made the danger real, that certified him as worthy to face it. To passengers he would say "No cause for alarm." Pichon is proud to be entrusted with these secrets of the profession. "Anyhow," the instructor is saying, "there's nothing dangerous about flying."

They are waiting for Mortier. Bernis fills his pipe. A mechanic is perched on an oil drum, his chin propped on his hands, staring absently at his foot as it beats time.

"Say, Bernis, weather's closing in!" The mechanic looks up.

The horizon has grown hazy. Two or three trees are outlined against the sky, but the fog is melting them into one. Bernis does not raise his head; he tamps steadily on his pipe. "I know. I don't like it." This is the day Mortier is due to get his license; he must have made a landing somewhere.

"Bernis, you ought to phone. . . ."

He phones. . . . "Took off at four-twenty. . . . No word since then?" . . .

"No word."

The colonel walks away.

Bernis stands, his closed fists resting on his hips. He looks defiantly at the fog that is falling gently, like a net, pressing the student, God knows where he is, down against the earth. "And Mortier, of all people . . . loses his head, flies like an ass . . . what a mess."

"Listen!" . . . No, just a car.

"Mortier, if you get out of this, I promise you a . . . I . . . I'm rooting for you, fellow."

"Bernis! Telephone!"

"Hello. . . . Who is the lunatic who's buzzing rooftops over in Donazelle? I'll tell you who it is. Some fool trying to kill himself.

"Damned fog, give the poor devil a break! . . . Oh, come on, why don't you get out your ladder and try to bag him!"

Bernis hangs up. Mortier has lost his bearings, obviously, and is looking for some landmark.

The fog is shifting and shelving like a watery archway. Visibility is less than thirty feet.

"Tell the orderlies to get the ambulance out here on the double. If they're not here in five minutes, they can count on two weeks K.P."

"There he is!" Every man is on his feet. Invisible and blind, Mortier is boring toward them. The colonel has rejoined the group. "My word, my word, my word." . . .

14

Between clenched teeth, Bernis mutters: "Cut your engine. Cut your engine, for the love of God! Cut! . . . You can't help but crash into something!"

Whatever it was, he must not have seen it. It didn't have to be more than thirty feet away, but no one ever knew for sure.

They run toward the crash. A few soldiers are already at the scene, drawn by this unexpected break in the day's routine. Some overly zealous noncoms, too, and a few senior officers whose authority of a sudden weighs heavily on their shoulders. The officer of the day is on hand, and he who has seen nothing is busy explaining everything. The colonel is there, fussing about. He, after all, plays the thankless role of father.

At last the pilot is dragged out from under the wreckage: face green, left eye bulging, teeth smashed. They lay him out on the grass and stand around him in a circle. "Maybe one could . . . ," the colonel says. "Maybe one could . . . ," a lieutenant echoes. And a noncom loosens the injured man's collar. It can do him no harm and it eases their consciences. "The ambulance? Where's the ambulance?" the colonel keeps repeating, groping among his training for some decision he might make now. "It's coming," they tell him, knowing nothing about it. He is satisfied. Then he cries "By the way . . ." and he rushes away—nowhere, just away.

The situation makes Bernis uncomfortable. He finds this circle of faces clustered around the dying man unseemly. "Let's get moving, fellows . . . move along, move along. . . ."

They walk off into the fog, through the vegetable gardens and orchards where this plane—a plane like any other plane—fell.

The student has understood one thing: when a man dies there's no fuss. He feels almost proud of his intimacy with death. He relives his flight with Bernis, his disappointment in the flatness of the earth. He would never have guessed that this presence had been lurking behind that calm. But it was there; quiet and unobtrusive, it had been there. It had lurked behind Bernis's smile, behind the mechanic's apathy, behind the foreground of sun and blue sky. He grasps Bernis by the arm. "I'll fly tomorrow, you know. . . . I'm not afraid."

But Bernis will not admire him: "Naturally. Tomorrow you'll do your turns."

And now Pichon learns something else. "They didn't seem very much upset—not that you have to make speeches."

"It was an accident on the job," Bernis replies.

Bernis is drunk.

This single-seater pursuit plane travels faster than lightning. Below, the earth is ugly: worn, threadbare, mended, and patched as far as the eye can see, parceled out in little bundles.

Thirteen thousand feet: Bernis is alone. He looks down at the earth, ribbed like a map of Europe. The yellow of wheatfields, the red of clover—the pride and passion of men—jostle each other, rigid and hostile. A thousand years of squabbles, jealousies, and lawsuits have drawn the boundary lines that fence in men's joy.

16

He must no longer feed his intoxication on the reveries that cradle and quicken his spirit. He must fuel it now from his power. He measures that power.

He picks up speed—his reservoir of energy—opens the throttle wide, pushes the joystick. The horizon tips, the earth slips back like a tide, the plane roars skyward. At the peak of the parabola, he flips over, and belly up, like a dead fish, he bobs and floats on the air.

Drowned in the sky, the pilot sees the earth above him fan out like a coastline, then tumble and spin. . . . He cuts his engine; the earth steadies and becomes motionless, perpendicular as a wall. The plane is plummeting, but Bernis gently pulls it up until the calm lake of the horizon spreads before him.

He banks, and the pressure blots him against his seat. Like a blister about to burst, the spars withstand the weight of the air. A torrent sweeps the horizon away and casts it back. The engine, ever obedient, growls, fades, rekindles. . . .

A dry snap—the left wing! The pilot has been dealt a treacherous trick, the air has been pulled out from under him. The plane shudders and spirals downward.

The horizon draws over his head like a veil. The revolving earth reaches out toward him, whipping its woodlands, its bell towers, its meadows through a giddy dance. The pilot sees a white villa, catapulted by the branch of a tree, sweep before his eyes. And as the sea rises to engulf the diver, the earth gushes toward the murdered pilot.

II.

NOBLEMAN...
BONDSMAN

This preface originally appeared in *Grandeur et Servitude de l'Aviation* by Maurice Bourdet, published by Corrêa, Paris, in 1933.

When you are flying the mail from Dakar to Casablanca, around two in the morning, you inch the black nose of your plane into a cluster of stars—I don't know their names, but they ride a bit to the right of the cusp of the Big Dipper. As they mount the curve of the sky, you exchange them for others, choose a new guidepost, so that you need not crane your neck. The night washes the visible world clear of all but the stars that reign over the black sands of the desert, and little by little it also cleanses your heart. The trivial worries that had seemed so urgent, the anger, the clouded desires and the jealousies are erased, and the real anxieties emerge. Then, as you slowly descend the stairway of the stars toward the dawn, you feel purged.

With his great talent and his great heart, Maurice Bourdet is trying to make us understand the nobility and servitude of the pilot's job. Here I would like to speak merely of what I think is essential in it.

The job has its grandeurs, yes. There is the exultation of arriving safely after a storm, the joy of gliding down out of the darkness of night or tempest toward a sun-drenched Alicante or Santiago; there is the swelling sense of returning to repossess one's place in life, in the miraculous garden of earth where there are trees and women and, down by the harbor, friendly little bars. When he has throttled his engine and is banking into the airport, leaving the somber cloud masses behind, what pilot does not break into song?

There is also drudgery. This, perhaps, is what makes the pilot love his job. To be roused unexpectedly from bed; to have to leave within the hour for Senegal; to have to renounce so much of life. . . . And then the engine failures over swampland, the forced marches over sand or snow. . . . Fate drops the pilot on some strange planet and somehow he must get out, must escape from the encircling mountains or sand or silence into the living world. Yes, there is always silence. When the mail plane does not come in on schedule, they wait an hour, a day, two days, but already the silence that separates the one man from those who still have hope is too dense. Many comrades who have never been heard from have sunk into death as if it were a snowbank.

Drudgery and grandeur, yes, but there is more. The pilot who is flying up to Casa ensconced in the heart of the night, whose dark nose cone balances delicately among the stars like the prow of a ship, is steeped in what is truly essential.

The cardinal event is the passing of night into day, and this the pilot surprises in its closest intimacy. He surprises day at her birth. He has always known it for a fact that the sky in the east lightens long before the sun rises, but only when he is aloft does he glimpse this fountain of light. He has witnessed a thousand and one dawns; he knows that the sky brightens. What he has not known is that the light wells up and flows across the sky as if it were gushing forth from a spring; he has not known the artesian well of day.

Day and night, mountain, sea, storm—in the midst of these primitive divinities, the airline pilot is guided by a simple morality and rediscovers the wisdom of the peasant.

The old-fashioned country doctor who travels through the evening from farmhouse to farmhouse to rekindle men's eyes, the solitary gardener whose hand knows how to bring roses into bloom—any man whose work brings him close to life and death draws wisdom from the nearness. Nobility also is found in danger. The pilot is far from the perils of the parade ground or any academic relish for risk. No one among the true comrades could fail to sense that such facile attitudinizing has in it something harmful to true courage and to the men who make danger their daily bread, who must battle hard to return.

What is essential? Maybe it is not the exhilaration or the strain or the danger but the point of view to which these things lift us. With his engine throttled and idling, the pilot drifts down toward the landing field, and from above surveys the city in which men dwell with all their afflictions, money worries, meannesses, envy, and rancour, and he feels pure, beyond attaint. If he has spent a hard night, he savors the joy of being alive. He is no laborer who is finishing his day's work only to lock himself up in the prison of some suburb. He is a

23

prince leisurely returning to his royal gardens. Green forests, blue rivers, rose-colored roofs are the treasures offered up to him. And the woman, still invisible behind the stones of the city below, who will come to life, who will grow to his stature, and whom he will love.

III.

MOSCOW

1935

Saint-Exupéry's visit to Russia, in April and May, 1935, followed a Mediterranean speaking tour he made as a representative of Air France, and preceded his attempt to break the Paris-Saigon flying-time record—a flight that ended in disaster when his Simoon crashed in the Libyan desert. Saint-Exupéry went to Moscow as special correspondent for *Paris-Soir*, arriving there in time for the May Day celebrations. His dispatches appeared on May 3, 14, 16, 19, 20, and 22, 1935.

1. Moscow Celebrates May Day

Moscow. MAY 3.—Two nights ago, on the eve of May Day, I walked through the streets of Moscow for several hours, watching the city prepare for its great holiday.

The town was transformed into a bustling shipyard. Crews of men were at work stringing lights across the façades of public buildings, festooning the walls with long scarlet banners and flags, setting up floodlights. In Red Square, relays of wheelbarrows trundled fresh cement to workers who were rapidly laying whole sections of new pavement. The streets pulsed with the peculiar excitement of night work, which turns labor into a kind of game, a muffled, thudding dance around a fire. Red banners masked the buildings from roof to street; they were spread so wide that they bellied out like sails in the wind and gave the whole holiday scene the semblance of a regatta. The city might have been preparing to set sail for some vast far-off horizon.

Passers-by, both men and women, paused to watch the work. The next day, these same men and women—four mil-

27

lion of them—came to march before Stalin as the whole city paid him homage.

Workmen were hoisting billboards as tall as statues on which his vigorous foreman's face had been rather crudely painted against a background of factories. As the crews were lifting these posters into place, I strolled around the Kremlin walls. Inside, that foreman was perhaps already asleep, or maybe other preparations were in the making there.

"Keep moving!" . . . Sentinels stand guard night and day around this forbidden zone where the Master lives. The whole circumference of the Kremlin walls is off limits to the loiterer. The strictest security measures surround this man.

Not only ramparts and sentinels protect this city within a city, but inside broad lawns extend, like sloping snares of greensward, from the outer walls to the somber inner buildings. No one could slip undetected into the silent stone-grass vacuum that contains Stalin.

One might almost imagine that he does not exist, so invisible is his presence. Yet the man who sleeps here tonight, shielded by guards and lawns and ramparts, quickens all Russia with his invisible presence; he acts on her like a fermenting yeast. But if he himself is rarely seen, his image is multiplied a hundred thousandfold along the streets of Moscow. Every shop window, every restaurant, every theater displays him; there is no wall that he does not dominate. I am beginning to sense a part of what lies behind this prodigious popularity.

At first, I think, the Russians felt he was a pitiless tyrant. Stalin weighed heavily on Russia. People tried to escape his control by fleeing abroad or by pilfering and other under-cover dealings. But Stalin hemmed the country in with the dictum "Stay where you are. . . . Build. . . . Famine and poverty are your enemies, and you must defeat them on the spot, defeat them by plowing the earth, carrying bricks. . . ." And so he led his people toward a promised land that he forced them to bring into being on the very site of the old exhausted earth they knew, rather than leading them on an exodus to some foreign fertile soil or with the mirages of some desperate adventure.

He possesses a strange authority. One day he decreed that no self-respecting man should neglect his appearance; an un-shaved face would be taken as a sign of laxness. The next day, factory foremen and department-store supervisors and uni-versity professors turned men away who appeared with a stubble. One can imagine the scenes:

Student: I didn't have time.

Professor: A good student finds time. It is a mark of respect for his teacher.

Thus, from one day to the next, Stalin pulled the country up one step out of slovenliness. It was achieved under the pressure of a command, of course, but how effectively! I have not seen one policeman, soldier, waiter, or pedestrian in Mos-cow who was not freshly shaved.

When the magic wand of the Five-Year Plan touches the Moscow uniform (the caps and work clothes worn by every-one here contribute a gray, rather gloomy tone to the landscape) the streets of the city will be brightened at one stroke. Is it too paradoxical to imagine that the day will come when, from the inner recesses of his Kremlin, Stalin will decree that a good, self-respecting proletarian must dress in the evening? And that Russia will sit down at table that night in a dinner jacket?

He holds such power, that invisible man sleeping in the Kremlin who will appear the next day before the people.

I had already learned, to my cost, that one does not with impunity flout this Russian deity simply because he is hidden away in his temple. On arriving, I discovered that I would not be granted a spectator's permit for Red Square on May Day. To obtain this I would have had to come to Moscow much earlier than I had, for each application involves a prolonged individual investigation and a rigorous weeding out of applicants. I have had too little time to set the vast administrative machinery in motion, and neither the embassy nor friends could do a thing. No one will be able to slip within the radius of a mile around Stalin unless his civilian status and antecedents have been checked, double-checked, and, for good measure, triple-checked.

When I tried to go out early on the morning of May first, I found the door of the hotel locked. It would be opened, I was informed, at four o'clock that afternoon. Until then, people without a permit were, in effect, prisoners.

I was wandering gloomily around the hotel when I heard the thunderstorm break overhead. They were planes, I realized. A thousand planes were descending on Moscow, and the earth trembled. I could not see a thing, but I could feel the weight of this iron hand bearing down upon the city. Somehow I had to get out and this time (by a sleight of hand I will not disclose) I made it.

I walked out into a kind of desert, for almost all normal life had been swept off the streets. Only a few children were playing here and there on the sidewalks. Looking up, I saw a steel triangle of Air Force squadrons pierce my narrow sector of vision and pass from sight. They were flying in rigid order, and each formation had the coherence of a tool. One after another, the dark masses rolled slowly overhead—a thousand planes!—with a deep-throated, solemn, undiminishing roar. It was a massive spectacle, impressive but also oppressive. As I leaned against a wall and stared up, I discovered that whereas a single squadron wings by like a great bird, a thousand planes rumble across the sky like a steamroller.

I walked down several deserted streets, was brought up short by several police barriers, and finally came to an avenue that was alive with demonstrators flowing by on their way to Red Square. The crowd reached for miles, and it was moving forward slowly and inexorably, like a great black wave. Like the march of a thousand planes, the march of a whole people has something pitiless about it, rather like unanimity in a jury. This rolling flood of dark-clothed figures—dingy despite the flutter of red flags—was almost blind in its power. And it was perhaps more impressive than a parade of troops. When soldiers march, they are doing a job; and, that job done, they become Tom and Dick again. But these marchers were absorbed to the very roots of their being; mind and body—even

31

their work clothes—struck me as imbued with an unwavering purpose. I stood by watching until presently the river stopped in its course.

It was a long halt. Very likely other streets had opened like locks into Red Square, so that these people had to wait. They waited in a glacial cold, for it had snowed again the night before. And all of a sudden a kind of miracle happened.

The miracle was a return to the human. This unified, solid mass suddenly melted into single human beings. Accordions struck up along the street. Several male choruses with their brass instruments were in the line of march; now they grouped themselves in circles and began to play. Partly to get warm, partly for the fun of it, partly perhaps to celebrate the holiday, people started to dance. Here on the threshold of Red Square, thousands upon thousands of men and women, their faces suddenly unfrozen and smiling, danced in circles. The whole street took on a festive, familial air, like any Paris suburb on a July 14 night.

A stranger spoke to me, offered me a cigarette. Another man proffered a light. The crowd was in high good spirits. . . .

Then, up ahead, figures began to eddy about. The chorusers tucked their instruments under their arms, banners were raised, and the lines reformed. A group leader tapped one woman demonstrator lightly on the head with his stick to bring her into line. It was the last individual, personal gesture. People became grave again as they resumed their march toward Red Square. They were reabsorbed into the crowd as one ready to appear before Stalin.

32

2. En Route to the U.S.S.R.

Moscow. MAY 14.—In my first dispatch I described May Day in Moscow, which was an outright surrender on my part to headline pressures. I should have begun by telling about my trip. A trip is like a preface; it prepares one to understand a new country. One can even learn something from the atmosphere aboard an international express. The train is not merely a convoy streaking through the countryside at night, it is a tool for gaining entry into strange premises. My train cut an unswerving path across a Europe torn by anxieties and hostility; it seemed to cross borders with ease, but I thought I might nonetheless detect some obscure sign that would reveal the rents in the fabric of Europe.

It was midnight and I lay in my compartment under the dim light of the night lamp, simply letting myself be borne along through the darkness. The sound of steadily clicking wheels reached me through the wood paneling and brass fixtures of my compartment like a pulse beat. Outside something

33

was flowing by unseen. Sound was my only clue. A rasping noise meant a bridge or tunnel wall. A station with an expanse of wide platforms was as silent as a bed of sand. At first, this was all I knew.

Hundreds of travelers were sleeping in these cars, all carried along as easily as I. Were they feeling a prick of anxiety, too? What I was going to look for I quite realized I might not find. I do not believe in local color. I have traveled enough to know how misleading it is. The extent to which it amuses or intrigues us measures the extent by which we are still judging a country from a foreigner's point of view. We have not yet understood its essence. The essence of a custom or ceremony is the flavor each imparts, the sense of life that each generates. If it possesses this power, then it seems to us, rather than picturesque, only simple and natural.

If only in a confused way, however, everyone has a sense of the profound nature of travel. For any man a trip must be a little like a woman moving toward him. She is lost in the crowd, and it is for him to discover her. At first, she is scarcely distinguishable from all the others. As he hovers on the brink of discovery, he may accost a thousand and one women, but he will have wasted his time if he cannot recognize the only vulnerable one. To travel is like that.

I was suddenly seized by a desire to make a tour of the little country in which I was locked up for three days, cradled in that rattle that is like the sound of pebbles rolled over and over by the waves; and I got up out of my berth. At one in the morning I went through the train in all its length. The sleeping cars were empty. The first-class carriages were empty. They put me in mind of the luxurious hotels on the Riviera that open in winter for a single guest, the last representative of an extinct fauna. A sign of bitter times.

But the third-class carriages were crowded with hundreds of Polish workmen who were being sent home from France. I made my way along those passages, stepping over sprawling bodies and peering into the carriages. In the dim glow cast by the night lamps into these barren and comfortless compartments, I saw a confused mass of people churned about by the swaying of the train, the whole thing looking and smelling like a barracks room. A whole nation returning to its native poverty seemed to sprawl there in a sea of bad dreams. Great shaven heads rolled on the cushionless benches. Men, women, and children were stirring in their sleep, tossing from left to right and back again as if they were being attacked by all the noises and jerkings that threatened them in their oblivion. They had not found the hospitality of a sweet slumber.

Looking at them, I told myself that they had lost half their human quality. These people had been knocked about from one end of Europe to the other by the economic currents. And now they had been torn from their little houses in the north of France, from their tiny garden plots, their three pots of geraniums that always stood in the windows of the Polish miner's families. I saw lying beside them pots and pans, blankets, curtains, bound into bundles badly tied and swollen with hernias.

Out of all that they had caressed or loved in France, out of everything they had succeeded in taming in their four or five years in my country—the cat, the dog, the geranium—they had been able to bring away with them only a few kitchen utensils, two or three blankets, a curtain or so.

A baby lay at the breast of a mother so weary that she seemed asleep. Life was being transmitted amid the shabbiness and the disorder of this journey. I looked at the father. A powerful skull as naked as a stone. A body hunched over in uncomfortable sleep, imprisoned in working clothes, all humps and hollows. The man looked like a lump of clay, like one of those sluggish and shapeless derelicts that crumple into sleep in our public markets.

And I thought: The problem does not reside in this poverty, in this filth, in this ugliness. But this same man and this same woman met one day. This man must have smiled at this woman. He may, after his work was done, have brought her flowers. Timid and awkward, perhaps he trembled lest she disdain him. And this woman, out of natural coquetry, this woman sure of her charms, perhaps took pleasure in teasing him. And this man, this man who is now no more than a machine for swinging a pick or a sledge-hammer, must have felt in his heart a delicious anguish. The mystery is that they should have become these lumps of clay. Into what terrible mold were they forced? What was it that marked them like this, as if they had been put through a monstrous stamping

36

machine? A deer, a gazelle, any animal grown old, preserves its grace. What is it that corrupts this wonderful clay of which man is kneaded?

I went on through these people whose slumber was as sinister as a den of evil. A vague noise floated in the air made up of raucous snores, obscure moanings, and the scraping of clogs as their wearers, broken on one side, sought comfort on the other. And always the muted accompaniment of those pebbles rolled over and over by the waves.

I sat down face to face with one couple. Between the man and the woman a child had hollowed himself out a place and fallen asleep. He turned in his slumber, and in the dim lamplight I saw his face. What an adorable face! A golden fruit had been born of these two peasants. Forth from this sluggish scum had sprung this miracle of delight and grace.

I bent over the smooth brow, over those mildly pouting lips. This is a musician's face, I told myself. This is the child Mozart. This is a life full of beautiful promise. Little princes in legends are not different from this. Protected, sheltered, cultivated, what could not this child become?

When by mutation a new rose is born in a garden, all the gardeners rejoice. They isolate the rose, tend it, foster it. But there is no gardener for men. This little Mozart will be shaped like the rest by the common stamping machine. This little Mozart will love shoddy music in the stench of night dives. This little Mozart is condemned.

I went back to my sleeping car. I said to myself: Their fate causes these people no suffering. It is not an impulse to charity

37

that has upset me like this. I am not weeping over an eternally open wound. Those who carry the wound do not feel it. It is the human race and not the individual that is wounded here, is outraged here. I do not believe in pity. What torments me tonight is the gardener's point of view. What torments me is not this poverty to which after all a man can accustom himself as easily as to sloth. Generations of Orientals live in filth and love it. What torments me is neither the humps nor the hollows nor the ugliness. It is the sight, a little bit in all these men, of Mozart murdered.

There was a knock at the door and someone called my name. Voices on a train at night seem to speak only of secret things, but when I opened the door, the porter, standing under the dim night lamp and swaying with the roll of the train, asked me what time I wanted to be awakened. What could be less mysterious, yet I felt all the empty spaces that separate human beings yawn between me and this neutral man. City people forget what a man is; he is reduced to his function, and he is a porter or a salesman or an inopportune neighbor. The best place for discovering what a man is is the heart of the desert. Your plane has broken down, and you walk for hours, heading for the little fort at Nutchott. You wait for the mirages of thirst to gape before you. But you arrive and you find an old sergeant who has been isolated for months among the dunes, and he is so happy to be found that he weeps. And you weep, too. In the arching immensity of the night, each tells the story of his life, each offers the other the burden of memories in which the human bond is discovered. Here two men can meet, and they bestow gifts upon each other with the dignity of ambassadors.

To reach the dining car I had to retrace my steps through the third-class cars. The night's vision of truth had vanished, and in the daylight the Poles seemed simply to be stranded there. They had pulled themselves together, blown their children's noses, put their bundles in order, and now they sat watching the countryside rush by and joking among themselves. One man was singing. Tragedy had evaporated. I understood that it is possible to live with a clear conscience by thinking of these people as they are. These gnarled hands would not know how to do more than labor with pick and ax. These people present no problem because, fashioned as they are by destiny, they seem to be their own destiny.

I should have been able to rejoice to watch them comfortably doling out their food from its greasy wrappings and taking their simple pleasure in the landscape that unrolled before them. I should have been appeased to tell myself that there was no social problem here. These faces were as closed as blocks of granite. But the magic of night had showed me, underneath the *gangue*, the child Mozart asleep. . . .

The dining car was knifing through farmland, the fields now impoverished and encircled by straggling tree clumps like mangy fur pieces; it was driving on into the heart of Germany, and today the dining car had become German. The waiters moved about with the cool politeness of great noble-

39

men. Why is it that the waiters, whether German, Polish, or Russian, all have this lordly air? Why is it that the moment you leave France you become aware of a slackness in France? Why do we have a slightly vulgar air of egalitarian complacency? Why are our people indifferent to their work, their function—in a word, to style? What is the root of this apathy? There is something symbolic in our small-town ceremonies. The unveiling of a monument, say. The minister arrives, he delivers a long harangue that he did not write, he eulogizes some sharp operator whom he never knew, and neither he nor the crowd believes a word he is saying. He is playing a game, but it is a game without stakes, a kind of benevolent farce.

Once beyond our borders, you feel that men live in terms of their function. The dining-car waiter, impeccably dressed, gives impeccable service. The minister deals with issues that concern his listeners. His words go to the heart of the matter. And if massive police protection surrounds the raising of the most minor statue, it is to smother subterranean fires. In this game the stakes are high.

But what, then, of that sense of fraternal ease you experience in France? What of the taxi driver whose very familiarity admits you into the circle of his intimates? What of the friendly, obliging waiters in the cafés on Rue Royale who know half of Paris and all its secrets, who will undertake to make the most personal phone calls for you or, in a pinch, lend you a few francs, who notice when the trees are in bud and greet old customers with the cheering announcement that spring is here at last?

Everything presents contradictions and conflicts. The agonizing dilemma is to discover where life is leading and to have to make a choice. I was thinking of that as I listened to the man across the table from me, a German. "Together France and Germany would be masters of the world," he was saying. "Why are the French so afraid of Hitler? He's the buffer between them and Russia, isn't he? All he's done is to give back to people here their freedom of action. He's one of the world's builders, one of those men whose names live on in the straight, broad avenues they've created. He stands for order."

At the next table there are some Spaniards who, like me, are on their way to Russia, and they're already afire with enthusiasm. I can hear snatches of their conversation—Stalin, Five-Year Plan, this launched, that flourishing. . . . The landscape has changed indeed! Once the frontiers of France are behind you, you care very little about spring and are perhaps more concerned with the destiny of mankind.

3. Moscow: Where Is the Revolution?

Moscow. MAY 16.—A half hour from the Russian border the onward rush of our express slowed to a crawl. I had already fastened my bags for we were to change trains, and I stood, with my forehead pressed against the window, staring at the countryside. All I would know of Poland was this air that mingled the scent of sand and dark fir trees. The memory I would take with me was the sharp whiff of a slightly briny beach.

The farther north one travels, the more color light acquires. In the tropics, the light is bright but without hue. There is the light, and under that light objects are black. Even the sky is black. Here objects were coming to life, beginning to gleam. A soundless, frozen fete glowed among the firs, for this somber tree takes light best, just as it allows fire to sweep through it like the wind. I thought of my forests in the Landes; they did not burn, they blew away.

The train pulled in slowly alongside the platform. Negoreloye. We had reached Russia.

What built-in prejudice made me look at once for signs of

dilapidation? The customs office could have served well as a ballroom; it was large, airy, with gilt decorations. The station restaurant came as an even greater surprise. A gipsy orchestra was playing softly behind potted plants for diners who sat comfortably at small tables. I found it hard to make reality fit my expectations, and so I became suspicious. This was all show, a front for the benefit of foreigners. Perhaps. But so is the Bellegarde customs, and the Bellegarde customs is as shabby as the courtroom in the prefecture of police of Paris.

I could easily imagine, that I was being hoodwinked, yes, but for the moment I was in no position to judge. I was a simple foreigner whose luggage was being examined, and I could only regret that it was being examined so properly. The man next to me, however, managed a show of temper: "You're in charge here, naturally, so I can't stop you from wrinkling my shirts, but. . . ." The inspector glanced at him indifferently and went on with his search. He was so indifferent that he did not even take a closer look, did not bother to display his authority. An image flashed through my mind: this single man was backed up by a hundred and sixty million others. One does sense a denseness about Russia, and that, I felt, was what made this man strong. My neighbor was floundering in this indifference, and his anger quickly burned out—which is pretty much what happened once to an army that was met here only by silence and snow.

Later, from my seat on the Moscow train, I tried to decipher the dark countryside. This was Russia, the country that none of us can discuss without an explosion of feeling. This was the country we know nothing about, perhaps because our feelings run so high or because the Soviet Union is so near. We know China better—or rather, we know better from what point of view to judge China. Hardly anyone disagrees about China. But when it is a matter of passing judgment on the Soviet Union, attitudes range from the extremes of admiration and hostility. It depends on your point of view, on which you value more, the creation of a new society or respect for the individual.

So far, however, I had encountered no problems. The door to the country had been opened to me by a pleasant-mannered customs official. And by a gipsy orchestra. And shortly after, in the dining car, by the most authentically polished and impeccable of headwaiters.

Morning produced that slight fever that accompanies imminent arrival by train. The countryside was already sprouting houses, and these houses were multiplying and inching closer together. Roads were running like the spokes of a wheel toward some invisible hub. A great knot was taking shape. It was Moscow, set like a magnet in the heart of its filings.

The train rounded a bend and suddenly there was the city, a monumental block. I counted seventy-one planes sweeping across the sky. My first image of Moscow was that of an enormous hive swarming with bees.

Georges Kessel was at the station. He called a porter, whereupon this new world continued to shed its ghosts. The porter was like all other porters; he picked up my bags, carried them to a cab, and put them inside. Before getting in, I looked around me. I saw a wide square, trucks rumbling across it, and I noted that the paving was a fine macadam. I saw some trams, strung together the way they are in Marseille, and then an altogether unexpected and cozy scene—an ice-cream vendor with soldiers and children crowding around his cart.

And so I have gone on to discover, little by little, how naive I was to have believed the tales I had been told. I started out on the wrong track. I had been waiting, searching for mysterious signs that are not here to be seen. Childishly, I had looked for the traces of revolution in the behavior of a porter or in the display in a store window. A two-hour walk dispelled those illusions. This is not where one must do one's searching. I will no longer be surprised by anything in the area of daily living. I will not be surprised when a young woman tells me, "Well, it isn't done. A young woman doesn't go into a bar alone in Moscow." Or, "Yes, a man will kiss a woman's hand in Moscow, but not everyone would find it the natural thing to do." Nor will I be surprised again if Russian friends cancel an invitation to lunch because their maid unexpectedly asked permission to visit her sick mother. I am discovering in terms of my own mistakes how the Russian experiment is being distorted. It is not in things such as these that one must look for the new Russia. It is elsewhere that one discovers how profoundly the soil has been turned and worked by the revolution. Yet, here too, it is still the paver who paves the streets, and the manager who directs the factory—and it is *not* the stevedore who commands the ship.

4. Crime and Punishment: Justice in the Soviet Union

Moscow. MAY 19.—The judge was touching on something basic, I felt, as we sat and talked in his chambers. He tried to clarify his point by picking up something I had just said.

"But, you see, it is not a matter of punishment," he said. "The problem is to correct." He was speaking so quietly that I had to lean forward to catch his words, and as he talked his hands were delicately molding an invisible clay. "The problem is rather one of correction."

Here, I thought, is a man who does not know anger. He does not pay his fellow man the tribute of recognizing that he exists; for the judge, a man constitutes good malleable clay. Furthermore, the judge is as little capable of tenderness as of anger. It is possible to discern the finished work latent within the rough clay, possible also to care deeply about it, but tenderness can be born only of respect for individualities. Tenderness builds its nest in little things, in the absurdities of a face, in personal crotchets. When we lose a friend, it is probably his faults that we mourn.

This judge does not permit himself to judge. He is like the doctor whom nothing can shock. He cures if he can. But because he serves the well-being of society before all else, he executes when he cannot cure. The prisoner's stammer or his surliness or his rheumatism—which are his humble bonds with the rest of us—do not buy this man's mercy.

I sense that there is here a great disregard for the individual but a great respect for Man, who is perpetuated through generations of individuals and whose stature must be increased.

Guilty? I thought. The word has no meaning here any more.

I am beginning to understand why in Russian law there is such emphasis on the death penalty and why, at the same time, no prison sentence may exceed ten years. And why there are all manner of ways for even this to be reduced. If the nonconformist will ever throw his lot in with society, he will do so before ten years are up. Why then prolong a punishment that will have lost its purpose?

We speak of the prisoner as "paying his debt to society." Every year of expiation goes toward settling this invisible account. The debt may be too large ever to be paid off, in which case the prisoner is denied the right of ever again becoming a man. The fifty-year-old convict is still paying for the twenty-year-old youth who committed murder in a moment of rage.

47

The judge was going on as if he were speaking to himself. "Suppose that it is a question of preventing crime. Say that common-law crime is on the increase and that the problem is to stamp out an epidemic. Then we take stronger punitive measures. When an army is on the verge of going to pieces, you must make an example of a defector, and you have recourse to the firing squad. Quite possibly, two weeks before, the same man would have been sentenced to three years of hard labor for some petty burglary, but now he pays for it with his life. However, we will have arrested the epidemic, we will have saved other men." He looked at me closely.

"To our way of thinking, it is not wrong, it is not immoral to punish severely and even brutally at a time of social crisis. On the other hand, it *is* immoral to imprison a man within a word. I mean, to act as if the murderer were inherently a murderer—by his very nature and for life, the way a Negro is always a Negro. The murderer is in reality a murdered man. A judge's hands are always shaping invisible clay.

"Correct. Not punish but correct," he said. "We have had some remarkable results."

I am going to try to translate his point of view into our terms. Imagine a gangster or a pimp and the particular worlds he lives in, each of which has its own laws, standards, loyalties, and cruelties. I admit that a man brought up in such a school cannot be changed into a shepherd. He would miss the adventure, the ambush; he would miss the night. He would also lack the opportunity to use whatever faculties his way of life had fostered in him. Decisiveness, courage, maybe the will

48

to dominate others. Despite all the fine speeches about the advantages of the virtuous life, he would feel diminished.

Life leaves its mark on us. Prostitutes bear the mark of their profession and they are not easily recuperable, for they suffer relatively little from the enervating, bitter hours of waiting, from the gray cold of early dawn, even from fear, much less from the coffee and roll at five o'clock in the morning, when one makes peace with the police and the hostile city, and when the whole network of threats that the night has spun is unraveled.

Who can explain the appeal of poverty? Nor will peace tempt these people, for they have been formed by war. Nor will a quiet conscience tempt them.

Here in Russia the miracle happens in this way. Their thieves and pimps and murderers are fished out of penal servitude and dispatched, with a few attendant rifles, to dig the canal that will join the White and Baltic seas. There they find adventure—and what adventure!

Their job is to dig a ditch, but, like toiling giants, to dig a ditch that runs from one sea to the other, that is as deep as a ravine, scaled to the measure of a seagoing vessel. To block landslides with cathedral-high scaffolding, to buttress the sides of a fault with whole forests of planks that snap like straws under the pressure of subterranean shiftings of earth. When night falls, they return to their camp under the watchful muzzles of carbines. And the weight of their fatigue spreads a cloak of silence over these people. But they make camp in the vanguard of their project, their faces turned forward toward still unconquered terrain. And little by little they are caught up in the game. They work in gangs directed by foremen and engineers of their own kind (you find all varieties of talent in a prison). In other words, they are governed by those among themselves who best knew how to impose a natural superiority.

"I grant you the foundations of your system of justice, sir. But the endless expansion, the surveillance of private lives, the domestic passport, the enslavement of the individual to the collective—these are the things we find intolerable."

And yet I believe I am beginning to understand these things, too. Here they have founded a new society, and now they are insisting not only that men respect its laws but that they truly live in this new world. They are insisting that men organize themselves in a social corpus not only by observing outward forms but by adhering to the idea of it in their hearts. When this has been accomplished, then and only then will the restrictions be relaxed. A friend told me a rather good story that may throw some light on this.

He missed his train, so he went into the waiting room in the station of a small provincial town and prepared to sit out the afternoon. He noticed bundles of clothing here and there, and dozens of other surprising things such as samovars, and he supposed that they belonged to other people who, like himself, were traveling long distances. As evening fell, he saw the owners of these bundles come, one by one, into the waiting room. They arrived in a leisurely way, as if they were coming home from work. They had shopped on the way, and now they set about cooking vegetables for their evening meal. The station took on the cozy atmosphere of a family boarding house. People were talking, singing, blowing children's noses. My friend went over to the stationmaster.

"What are these people doing?"

"They're waiting," the stationmaster said.

"Waiting for what?"

"Permission to leave."

"To leave for where?"

"To leave, to take the train."

The stationmaster saw nothing surprising in this. They simply wanted to leave. It didn't matter where. To fulfill their destiny. To discover new stars, perhaps, having found their old stars burned out. My friend's first reaction was to admire their patience. He had found two hours in that waiting room unbearable; three days of it would have driven him mad. But these people were singing softly, bending tranquilly over their samovars. He went back to the stationmaster.

"How long have they been waiting?"

The man pushed back his cap, scratched his head, and then, after almost visible mental arithmetic, he said, "Must be five or six years now."

The Russians are part nomad. They are not deeply attached to where they live; they are haunted by the old Asian urge to set out in a caravan under the stars. They are a people who have forever been setting out in search of something—God, truth, the future. The houses that other men cherish make them feel tied down, and they are relieved to be quit of them.

It is hard to understand this detachment if one comes here from France, where the small house spinning its skein of woolly smoke into the still country air is so imperious a pole. Where the sheriff armed with a dispossess notice is assaulting a creature of flesh and blood and sundering a hundred tender, invisible bonds. Who could ever imagine people in the north of France camping out in their stations, intoxicated by the call of Provence? The man who lives in the north of France loves his fog abidingly. But here. . . .

Here they love the wide world. Perhaps they do truly inhabit this dream, and so must be taught about the earth, about the concrete. The government is fighting these eternal pilgrims. It is struggling to check the inner impulse of men who have glimpsed a star. It must prevent their setting off to the north, to the south, at the mercy of invisible tides. Now that the Revolution has been won, it must prevent their striking out for some other new social order. Is this not, after all, the country where the stars ignite fires?

So houses are built to tempt these nomads. Apartments are not rented, they must be bought. The domestic passport is made obligatory. Men who lift their eyes too high toward the dangerous signals of heaven are shipped to Siberia, where winter temperatures fall to a paralyzing 140° below zero.

Perhaps they are indeed creating a new man who will be stable and who will love his factory and his community as the gardener in France loves his garden.

5. Tragedy Strikes the *Maxim Gorki*

Moscow. MAY 20.—The *Maxim Gorki*, the world's largest airplane, has crashed. While maneuvering into position for a landing, the *Maxim Gorki* was rammed by a pursuit plane flying at more than two hundred and fifty miles an hour.

According to some witnesses, the pursuit plane sheared off a wing; others claim that it crashed into the main engine. All agree, however, that the great ship exploded as if struck by lightning. In a kind of slow motion, wings, engines, and fuselage disintegrated into a black cloud and seemed to float to earth. Observers say it was like witnessing a steep landslide or watching a torpedoed vessel slowly submerge and sink.

Fragments of the airship, which weighed forty-two tons, struck a frame house. The building was swept by flames and was completely demolished, killing all the inhabitants. Twelve crewmen, including the famous pilot Juroff, also perished, bringing the total number of victims in this air disaster to forty-eight.

The *Maxim Gorki*, which was the pride of the Russian air

fleet, had a wingspread of 210 feet, and measured some 114 feet in length. Its eight engines, three of which were located in either wing, developed 7000 horsepower. The plane had a cruising speed of one hundred and sixty miles an hour. It was equipped with a powerful loudspeaker, and as it descended through the clouds, it could speak above the roar of its motors to those listening on the ground.*

Just the evening before the disaster occurred, I flew aboard the *Maxim Gorki*. It was the first time—it was also the last—that a foreigner has been granted this privilege. I had been kept waiting a long time for the necessary permission, and only yesterday afternoon, after I had given up all hope, did I finally receive it. I took a seat in the one of two passenger lounges that was located in the very nose of the plane, so that I could watch the takeoff. The ship vibrated powerfully, and then I felt this forty-two-ton colossus lift itself into the air with what to me seemed amazing ease.

While we were circling back toward Moscow, I took a walk. "Walk" is the only word for it, for as we were flying along I inspected eleven of the plane's major compartments. These were connected by a network of automatic telephones, which was supplemented by a pneumatic-tube system for the transmission of written orders. The proportions of the plane

* The *Maxim Gorki* was a propaganda plane, equipped not only with a loudspeaker apparatus but with a film-projection room, presses capable of printing pamphlets and two-page papers, etc. It traveled widely in the Soviet Union, in even remote areas, offering Russians dramatic evidence of the growing technological capacity of their new nation.—Ed.

54

seemed all the more gigantic because the cabins were placed not only along the length of the fuselage but also in the nearer wing areas. I ventured down the corridor in the left wing and peered through the doors opening off it. They were variously cabins or engine rooms, real engine rooms in the sense that each engine was separately housed. An engineer joined me and showed me the electric-power plant. With its twelve-kilowatt capacity, this supplied power for the radio-communications system, the loudspeaker, certain takeoff and landing equipment, not to mention eighty light outlets distributed throughout the plane.

My inspection lasted fifteen minutes, and I felt as if I were enclosed in the belly of a torpedo, for not once did I see daylight. I was immersed in the ceaseless, heavy vibration of the engines. I passed by telephone operators, noticed beds in some cabins, met mechanics in blue overalls. My surprise was complete when I came upon a young woman typing quietly in a private office.

Then I returned to the light. Moscow was slowly revolving below us. The captain, sitting in one corner of the lounge, was telephoning orders I couldn't hear to his pilots. The radio-receiving post sent him occasional messages by the pneumatic tube. My impression was of a complex, highly organized group activity such as I had never experienced in my own flying.

I sank down into a chair and closed my eyes. Through the back of the seat I felt the gentle massage of eight engines. From head to foot I felt this pulsing life flow through my body. In my mind's eye I saw the generator delivering current and felt again the heat of those engine rooms that were like steam baths. I opened my eyes.

Blue light poured through a large window in the salon; I might have been enjoying a distant view from the balcony of a luxury hotel. The unity of the average plane where the pilot's station, his instruments, and the passengers' cabin are all one was broken here. Here you passed from the kingdom of the machine to the realm of leisure and dreams.

And the next day, the *Maxim Gorki* was no more. Its loss seems to be considered here as cause for national mourning. In addition to the pilot, Juroff, and the ten crew members—*la crème des hommes*—and the thirty-five passengers (all workers from the Tfagi factory who had been chosen to share in this flight in recognition of their work in the aereonautical plant), the U.S.S.R. has lost the finest proof she possessed of the vitality of her young industrial potential.

However, technicians with whom I have spoken seem to take some slight comfort in one thing, which is that the giant was felled by a senseless accident. The tragedy did not result from errors in the engineers' calculations, inexperience on the part of the factory workers, or any mechanical flaw. At a bloody crossroads in its peaceful flight, the *Maxim Gorki* was struck down because it lay in the path, as tautly drawn as the trajectory of a bullet, of a blind pursuit plane.

6. A Visit to the Past: Ten Tipsy Old Ladies at Home in Moscow

Moscow. MAY 22.—I checked the address again—No. 30—and stopped in front of a large, mournful house. Beyond the entrance, I saw a succession of courtyards and smaller buildings. Could any prison be gloomier, I thought, but then I reminded myself that this is a part of Moscow that is dying. Some day this termitarium will be demolished, and a towering white apartment house will rise on its foundations.

The population of Moscow has grown by almost three million in only a few years. Housing is quite inadequate, people are crowded into old buildings that have been broken up into small flats, and there they wait for new quarters to be completed. The procedure for obtaining a new apartment is simple enough. A group of history professors, say, or a group of cabinetmakers forms a cooperative. The government advances funds that the members contract to repay on a monthly basis. The cooperative forwards its building order to the appropriate state construction agency. Each member has

57

A Sense of Life

already reserved his apartment, discussed its layout, even chosen the colors he wants for his walls. Meanwhile, he waits patiently in drab, furnished rooms—the antechamber to a better life—knowing that it is only a temporary arrangement. New buildings are going up all the time but people must wait, much the way pioneers in a new country must live in shacks until they can build homes for themselves.

I have visited some modern apartments where the owners can enjoy a normal private life again. Now I wanted to see the other side of the picture, for many vestiges of the dark days of the past still survive. That was why I was reconnoitering No. 30. I went about it almost furtively, because I still half believed in those "agents" that are said to shadow the footsteps of all foreigners. I half expected one to loom up now and bar me from some jealously guarded secret of the Soviet Union. However, no one seemed to be paying any unwelcome attention to me when I walked into this anthill. I spoke to the first person I met and asked where I could find tenant so-and-so, whom I wanted to surprise, although I was coming as a complete stranger.

"Can you tell me where Mlle. Xavier lives?"

The first person I had met happened to be a generously built matron, who apparently took an immediate fancy to me. A flood of words poured forth, not one of which I understood. I don't speak Russian. I timidly tried to convey this, whereupon she responded with a host of additional explanations. I did not dare offend such a friendly soul by walking off, so I tapped my ear to indicate that I did not understand

58

her. This she took to signify that I was deaf, and she repeated her directions at the top of her lungs.

There was nothing for it but to take a chance, so I walked up the first stairway I came to and rang the first bell I saw. I was ushered into the apartment, and the man who had admitted me asked me something in Russian. I answered him in French. He studied me at some length, turned on his heel, and disappeared. I waited. I noticed a dozen things around me: a coat rack laden with coats and caps, a pair of shoes tossed on to a cupboard, a samovar perched on a valise. I heard a child crying somewhere, people laughing, a gramophone playing, doors opening and closing in the bowels of the house. I was as alone as any burglar in this strange apartment. Presently the man reappeared. He was accompanied by a housewife drying her soapy hands on her apron. She questioned me in English; I answered in French. At this, they looked downcast and both vanished through the door to the landing. I could hear sounds of a confabulation that grew more and more animated.

From time to time the door opened and strangers peered in at me perplexedly. Then apparently some decision was taken, for the whole house came alive. I heard people calling to each other and running up and down the stairs, and finally the door was flung wide. A third person came in and the chorus, massed behind him on the landing, obviously pinned great hopes on this candidate. He came up to me, bowed, and spoke to me in Danish. Now we were all discouraged.

In the midst of such widely shared dejection, I could not

59

help but think wryly of the trouble I'd taken to slip into the building unobserved. The flock of tenants and I were staring at each other despondently when a specialist in a fourth language was produced—and it was she, Mlle. Xavier herself. She looked rather like the wicked fairy, thin and bent and wrinkled but with sparkling eyes. She made neither head nor tail of my being there, but she invited me to her apartment.

And all those friendly people, rejoicing that finally they had rescued me, went their several ways.

I must confess that I was rather moved by my visit. There are, it seems, some three hundred Frenchwomen, from sixty to seventy years old, lost like so many gray mice in this city of four million inhabitants. They had been the teachers or governesses of the daughters of the old regime, and they have survived the revolution. Strange times! Their old world crashed around them like a temple. The revolution destroyed the strong and scattered the weak to the four corners of the earth, like the playthings of a storm, but it did not touch three hundred French governesses. They were too modest, too retiring, too correct. They had made themselves invisible for so long, following in the wake of their glamorous charges.

They taught these girls the graces of the French language, which their lovely pupils then gracefully employed to snare fiancés among the imperial guard. How could the governesses have dreamed that style and spelling held any such secret power, never having thought to apply them to the purposes of love? They taught deportment and music and dancing as well. These secrets fostered in them only a prim correctness but caused gaiety and light to bloom in their young pupils. And the governesses grew old in their black dresses, sober and strict, present but invisible, like virtue and duty and good breeding. And the revolution that cut down their flowering charges had not—at least not in Moscow—ruffled a hair of these gray mice.

Mlle. Xavier was seventy-two, and Mlle. Xavier wept. I was the first Frenchman to be in her house in thirty years. She said, for the nth time, "If I'd only known . . . if I'd only known, I could have made you so comfortable here." I glanced at the open door, and envisaged all the strangers who occupied the same apartment and who would be turning in reports by the dozen on our conversation. (I was still very romantic.) Mlle. Xavier laid this legend to rest: "I've left the door open on purpose," she said confidentially. "It's so wonderful that you've come to visit me. My neighbors will all be jealous."

She opened the cupboard noisily, made sure that the glasses tinkled, set a bottle of Madeira and a plate of little cakes down on the table with a bang. Then she clinked the glasses together and banged the bottle down again. The music of this orgy must be heard.

I listened while she talked. I had asked her about the revolution because I was curious to know what her point of view would be. What does a revolution mean to a gray mouse?

How does the mouse survive when everything is tumbling down around its ears?

"A revolution," my hostess observed, "a revolution is very trying, you know."

Mlle. Xavier had lived on the French lessons she gave to the daughter of a cook in exchange for one meal a day. Every day she had traveled the whole way across Moscow. To make a little pocket money, she used to sell on the way sundry possessions that elderly people gave her to dispose of for them—lipsticks, gloves, opera glasses.

"It was not legal," Mlle. Xavier confessed. "It was speculation. Quite irregular."

She told me about the darkest day of the civil war. That morning, she had been given some neckties to sell. Neckties to sell on such a day! But Mlle. Xavier saw neither soldiers nor machine gunners nor corpses. She was much too busy making a few pennies on the ties, which, she told me, created a sensation.

Poor little old governess. Social revolution passed her by just as love had. Adventure wanted no part of her. Who knows, perhaps on the old pirate ships there were aging, meek spinsters who took no notice of what went on around them because they were too busy mending the pirates' shirts!

However, one day she was picked up in a raid and thrown into some dark prison along with two or three hundred other suspects. Armed soldiers marched the prisoners one by one to the interrogation that was sorting the living from the dead.

"Half the prisoners," she told me, "were sent from the interrogation to the prison underground."

Well, once again adventure put on its most debonair face for her. Stretched out on a ledge above those black-mouthed pits that sank down to eternity, for her supper Mlle. Xavier was given a chunk of bread and three pralines. The three pralines rather strikingly bespeak the impoverishment of a whole people. They reminded me of the mahogany piano, a concert grand, that one of Mlle. Xavier's friends sold around that time for three francs. Yet the pralines also evoked all the savor of play and of childhood.

Adventure was treating Mlle. Xavier like a child. She, however, was devoured by worry. To whom could she entrust the eiderdown quilt she had acquired just before being arrested? That night she slept with it clutched to her; when she was called for cross-examination she would not let it out of her hands, and it was with this billowing quilt clasped to her tiny person that she appeared before her judges.

Not even the judges had taken her too seriously. Mlle. Xavier's recollection of her examination breathed indignation. Several men were sitting at a big kitchen table, surrounded by soldiers. The presiding judge checked her papers with a weariness born of a sleepless night. And then this man, whose presence one left to take the inexorable fork toward life or toward death, this man had scratched his ear and asked her diffidently, "I have a twenty-year-old daughter, Mademoiselle. Would you be willing to give her French lessons?"

And Mlle. Xavier, clasping her eiderdown to her bosom,

63

had answered with crushing dignity: "You have arrested me. Decide my case. Tomorrow, if I am still alive, we can discuss the matter of your daughter." And to me she added, her eyes snapping, "They didn't dare look at me, not a man among them. They just looked sheepish."

I did not disturb such adorable illusions. Man perceives in the outer world only what he bears within him. It calls for a certain breadth of imagination to confront the pathetic and accept its message.

I thought of the story the wife of a friend had told me. She had managed to get a place aboard the last White Russian ship to leave Sevastopol—or maybe it was Odessa—before the Reds arrived. The little vessel was filled to overflowing. Any additional weight would have capsized it, and it was slowly drawing away from the pier. Two worlds were already severed, and the separation, although slight, was irreparable.

Caught in the crowd in the stern of the boat, the young woman was looking back at the shore. For two days, the defeated Cossacks had poured down out of the mountains, and still they were arriving in an inexhaustible flood. But now there were no more ships. As the men reached the pier, they leaped from their horses, cut the animals' throats, ripped off their weapons and their dolmans, and plunged into the sea to swim to the safety of that last small ship, which was still so near. But other men with carbines were stationed in the stern with orders to prevent their clambering aboard. Every rifle shot caused a red star to burst on the surface of the sea, and soon the whole port was flowering with stars. Yet with the obsessive stubbornness of a nightmare, the Cossacks surged onto the pier, leaped from their horses, cut the animals' throats, and swam out toward the blossoming red stars. . . .

In the evening Mlle. Xavier summoned ten elderly French-women just like herself to the finest of their various lodgings. It was a charming apartment, which the owner herself had painted. I supplied the port, the wine, and liqueurs. We all got a little tipsy and sang old songs. Their childhood came back to them and they wept. Youth returned to their hearts and they called me *chéri*. I was a kind of Prince Charming, drunk on glory and vodka and surrounded by lots of little old ladies who kept kissing my cheeks.

Presently an exceedingly grave personage made his appearance. A rival. He came every evening, it seemed, to drink tea, talk French, and eat *petits fours*. Tonight, however, he sat down at the far end of the table, austere and bitter.

The little old ladies were eager to show him off in all his splendor. "He's Russian," they told me. "And do you know what he did?"

I didn't know. I guessed. The visitor assumed an increasingly modest air. Modest and forebearing. The modest bearing of a great gentleman. But they flocked around him and urged him on: "Tell our French friend what you did in 1906."

My rival played with his watch chain. He kept the ladies

dangling, too. Finally he gave in, turned to me, and very casually, but very clearly, he said, "In 1906, I played roulette in Monaco."

And the little old ladies, triumphant, burst into applause.

Around one o'clock in the morning I had to leave. I was escorted with much fanfare to a taxi. On either arm, I had a little old lady who was staggering ever so slightly. That evening I was the duenna.

Mlle. Xavier whispered in my ear, "Next year I will have my own apartment and we will all meet at my house. It will be so pretty, you'll see. I've started to embroider my doilies already." She leaned nearer. "You'll come to see me before the others? I'll be the first, won't I?"

Next year, Mlle. Xavier will be only seventy-three. She will have her own apartment. She will begin to live.

IV.

BARCELONA

1936

Saint-Exupéry's attempt to break the Paris-Saigon flight record ended with a disastrous crash in the Libyan desert, and he returned from Egypt low in spirits and heavily in debt. When the Spanish Civil War broke out, *l'Intransigeant* asked him to go to Spain as their special correspondent. He agreed, and left for Spain by plane in early August, 1936. His dispatches deal with Barcelona and his own overwhelming experiences on the Lérida front. They were published in *l'Intransigeant* on August 12, 13, 14, 16, and 19, 1936.

1. In a Civil War, the Firing Line Is Invisible

BARCELONA. AUGUST 12.—Flying west from Lyon, I veered left in the direction of the Pyrenees and Spain. Below me floated fleecy white clouds, summer clouds, clouds made for amateur flyers in which great gaps opened like skylights. Through one of these windows I could see Perpignan lying at the bottom of a well of light.

I was flying solo, and as I looked down on Perpignan I was daydreaming. I had spent six months there once while serving as test pilot at a nearby airdrome. When the day's work was done I would drive into this town where every day was as peaceful as Sunday. I would sit in a wicker chair within sound of the café band, sip a glass of port, and look idly on at the provincial life of the place, reflecting that it was as innocent as a review of lead soldiers. These pretty girls, these carefree strollers, this pure sky. . . .

But here came the Pyrenees. The last happy town was left behind.

Below me lay Figueras—and Spain. This was where men killed one another. What was most astonishing here was not the sight of conflagration, ruin, and signs of man's distress—it was the absence of all these. Figueras seemed no different from Perpignan. I leaned out and stared hard.

There were no scars on that heap of white gravel, that church gleaming in the sun, which I knew had been burnt. I could not distinguish its irreparable wounds. Gone was the pale smoke that had carried off its gilding, had melted in the blue of the sky its altar screens, its prayer books, its sacerdotal treasures. Not a line of the church was altered. This town, seated at the heart of its fan-shaped roads like a spider at the center of its silken trap, looked very much like the other.

Like other towns, this one was nourished by the fruits of the plain that rose along the white highways to meet it. All that I could discern was the slow gnawing which, through the centuries, had swallowed up the soil, driven away the forests, divided up the fields, dug out these life-giving irrigation ditches. Here was a face unlikely to change much, for it was already old. A colony of bees, I said to myself, once it was established so solidly within the boundaries of an acre of flowers, would be assured of peace. But peace is not given to a colony of men.

Human drama does not show itself on the surface of life. It is not played out in the visible world, but in the hearts of men. Even in happy Perpignan a victim of cancer walled up behind his hospital window goes round and round in a circle striving helplessly to escape the pain that hovers over him like a relentless kite. One man in misery can disrupt the peace of a city. It is another of the miraculous things about mankind that there is no pain nor passion that does not radiate to the ends of the earth. Let a man in a garret but burn with enough intensity and he will set fire to the world.

Gerona went by, Barcelona loomed into view, and I let myself glide gently down from the perch of my observatory. Even here I could see nothing out of the way, unless it was that the avenues were deserted. Again there were devastated churches which, from above, looked untouched. Faintly visible was something that I guessed to be smoke. Was that one of the signs I was seeking? Was this a scrap of evidence of that nearly soundless anger whose all-destroying wrath was so hard to measure? A whole civilization was contained in that faint golden puff so lightly dispersed by a breath of wind.

I am quite convinced of the sincerity of people who say: "Terror in Barcelona? Nonsense. That great city in ashes? A mere twenty houses wrecked. Streets heaped with the dead? A few hundred killed out of a population of a million. Where did you see a firing line running with blood and deafening with the roar of guns?"

I agree that I saw no firing line. I saw groups of tranquil men and women strolling on the avenue. When, on occasion, I ran against a barricade of militiamen in arms, a smile was often enough to open the way before me. I did not come at once upon the firing line. In a civil war the firing line is invisible; it passes through the hearts of men. And yet, on my very first night in Barcelona I skirted it.

71

I was sitting on the pavement of a café, sipping my drink, surrounded by lighthearted men and women, when suddenly four armed men stopped where I sat, stared at a man at the next table, and without a word pointed their guns at his stomach. Streaming with sweat, the man stood up and raised leaden arms above his head. One of the militiamen ran his hands over his clothes and his eyes over some papers he found in the man's pockets, and ordered him to come along.

The man left his half-emptied glass, the last glass of his life, and started down the road. Surrounded by the squad, his hands stuck up like the hands of a man going down for the last time. "Fascist!" A woman behind me said it with contempt. She was the only witness who dared betray that anything out of the ordinary had taken place. Untouched, the man's glass stood on the table, a mute witness to a mad confidence in chance, in forgiveness, in life. I sat watching the disappearance in a ring of rifles of a man who five minutes before, within two feet of me, had crossed the invisible firing line.

2. Anarchists and Their Ways: Street Scenes in Barcelona

BARCELONA. AUGUST 13.—A friend told me he was walking down a deserted street one evening when a militiaman called out to him, "Keep to the pavement!"

My friend's mind was on something else and he paid no attention, whereupon the militiaman raised his rifle and fired. He missed, but the bullet bored through the man's hat. Recalled in this fashion to a due regard for a gun, he moved over onto the sidewalk.

The militiaman was taking a second aim. Now he hesitated, lowered his rifle, and growled, "What's the matter? You deaf, or something?"

The tone of this reproach strikes me as utterly wonderful.

Without question, the city is in the hands of the anarchists. Groups of five or six stand guard at street corners and in front of the hotels, or they race through the city at sixty miles an hour in their requisitioned Hispanos.

The morning the revolt started, armed with nothing but knives, they charged a combination of artillerymen and machine gunners. They captured the artillery. Then they seized the supplies of guns and ammunition in the barracks and proceeded, naturally enough, to turn the city into a small fortress.

They control the city's water, gas, electricity, and transportation. On my morning walk, I see them busily putting the finishing touches to their barricades. You find all kinds, from simple walls of paving stones to double-ringed ramparts.

I glanced over one wall. There they were. They had dragged furniture belonging to some board of directors from the building next door, and comfortably ensconced in red leather chairs, were preparing for their civil war.

The men in my hotel are busy flying up and down the stairs.

"What's going on?"

"We're studying the lay of the land."

"Why?"

"We're setting up a machine gun on the roof."

"Why?"

A shrug is my answer.

This morning a rumor is making the rounds of the town. The government, so the story runs, is going to make an attempt to disarm the anarchists. They will soon give this idea up, I think.

Yesterday I took some snapshots of our garrison (every hotel has one of its own), and earlier today I was looking for one tall, dark-haired fellow, to give him a print of his photo.

"I've got his photo. Where is he?"

The man looked at me, scratched his head, and then, with a note of regret, said: "Well, we had to shoot him. . . . He'd denounced somebody as a fascist. So we shot the fascist. . . . But then this morning we discovered he was no fascist at all, just after the same girl."

They have their own sense of justice.

I was walking along the avenue around one o'clock at night when someone shouted "Halt!" I watched some rifles move from the shadows toward me.

"No farther. Not allowed."

"Why not?"

My papers were examined under the street light, then handed back to me.

"You can go on, but watch out. There may be some shooting around here."

"What's going on?"

No answer.

An artillery convoy came rumbling slowly down the street.

"Where are they going?"

"They're leaving for the front."

I did want to see them take off in the heart of night, so I tried cajoling the anarchists. "The station's awfully far away and it's raining. You don't suppose you could lend me a car, do you?"

A hand waved, and a man took off. He came back at the wheel of a requisitioned Delage.

"We'll drive you over. . . ." And, escorted by three rifles, I drove off to the station.

They are a strange breed and I still don't understand them. Tomorrow I will make them talk when I go to see their top man, Garcia Olivier.

3. Civil War: It Is Not a War, It Is a Disease

BARCELONA. AUGUST 14.—My guides were anarchists. They led me to the railway station where troops were being entrained. Far from the platforms built for tender farewells, we were walking in a desert of signal towers and switching points, stumbling in the rain through a labyrinthine yard filled with blackened goods wagons where tarpaulins the color of lard were spread over carloads of stiffened forms. This world had lost its human quality, had become a world of iron, and therefore uninhabitable. A ship remains a living thing only so long as man with his brushes and oils swabs an artificial layer of light over it. Leave them to themselves a couple of weeks, and the life dies out of your ship, your factory, your railway—death covers their faces. After six thousand years the stones of a temple still vibrate with the passage of man; but a little rust, a night of rain, and this railway yard is eaten away to its very skeleton.

Here are our men. Cannon and machine guns are being

77

respected? This body that clothes the spirit, that moves with grace and boldness, that knows love, that is apt for self-sacrifice—no one now so much as thinks of giving it decent burial.

I thought of our respect for the dead. I thought of the white sanatorium where the light of a man's life goes quietly out in the presence of those who love him and who garner as if it were an inestimable treasure his last words, his ultimate smile. How right they are! Seeing that this same whole is never again to take shape in the world. Never again will be heard exactly that note of laughter, that intonation of voice, that quality of repartee. Each individual is a miracle. No wonder we go on speaking of the dead for twenty years.

Here, in Spain, a man is simply stood up against a wall, and he gives up his entrails to the stones of the courtyard. You have been captured. You are shot. Reason: your ideas were not our ideas.

This entrainment in the rain is the only thing that rings true about their war. These men stand round and stare at me, and I read in their eyes a mournful sobriety. They know the fate that awaits them if they are captured. I begin to shiver with the cold, and I observe of a sudden that no woman has been allowed to see them off.

The absence of women seems to me right. There is no place here for mothers who bring children into the world in ignorance of the faith that will some day flare up in their sons, in ignorance of the ideologist who, according to his lights, will prop up their sons against a wall when they have come to their twenty years of life.

4. In Search of a War

BARCELONA. AUGUST 16.—I landed in Lérida late in the day and spent the night there before leaving the next morning for the front. The town is nearer the actual fighting than Barcelona—the front is only some twelve miles away—but it seemed more relaxed. Cars were moving through the streets at normal speeds, and not a single doorway I passed confronted me with the muzzle of a gun thrusting from the shadow. In Barcelona, twenty thousand index fingers are hooked around twenty thousand triggers twenty-four hours a day. Cars bristling with rifles hurtle through the streets night and day like miniature flying fortresses. Barcelona has become one huge target. Here enemy rifles are aimed virtually at the town's heart, but people have stopped paying much attention and go quietly about their business.

I did not see a single man walk down a Lérida street carrying a drawn revolver. I noticed none of the slightly ostentatious war gear that Barcelona men wear with studied casualness—as if they were carrying a flower or a pair of gloves.

Lérida is a front-line town and the people know it. They have no need to play at death games.

They are alert, nonetheless. When I checked in at my hotel, I was told: "Be sure you close your shutters. There's a militiaman stationed across the street after dark with orders to shoot out any lights that show through."

We went up by motor into the war zone. Barricades became more frequent, and from place to place we had to negotiate with revolutionary committees. Passes were valid only from one village to the next.

"Are you trying to get closer to the front?"

"Exactly."

The chairman of the local committee consulted a large-scale map.

"You won't be able to get through. The rebels have occupied the road four miles ahead. But you might try swinging left here. This road ought to be free. Though there was talk of rebel cavalry cutting it this morning."

It is very difficult in these early days of the revolution to know one's way about in the vicinity of the front. There are loyal villages, rebel villages, neutral villages, and they shift their allegiance between dawn and dark. This tangle of loyal and rebel zones made me think the push must be pretty weak. It certainly bore no resemblance to a line of trenches cutting off friend from enemy as cleanly as a knife. I felt as if I were walking in a bog. Here the earth was solid beneath our feet;

82

there we sank into it. We moved in a maze of uncertainty. Yet what space, what air between movements! These military operations are curiously lacking in density.

Outside one village we passed a wheezing threshing machine. The men were caught against the sun in a halo of golden chaff. They were working to provide bread for other men, and they smiled broadly at us as we drove by. It startled me to come upon such a peaceful scene, but apparently death hardly interferes with life here. I was reminded of the expression "one killer every square mile." Faced with the fraternal killers in this war, one is put to it to know who tends this land of vines, who reaps the harvest. The steady, singing beat of the thresher followed us a long way down the road, as tireless as the human heart.

Once again we reached a point beyond which we were told we could not advance. Six rifles and a low wall of paving stones blocked the road. Four men and two women lay stretched on the ground behind the wall. I made a mental note that the women did not know how to hold a rifle.

"This is as far as you can go."

"Why?"

"Rebels."

We got out of the car and sat down with the militiamen upon the grass. They put down their rifles and cut a few slices of fresh bread.

"Is this your village?" we asked.

"No, we are Catalans, from Barcelona. Communist party."

One of the girls stretched herself and sat up on the barricade, her hair blowing in the wind. She was rather thickset, but young and healthy. Smiling happily she said: "I am going to stay in this village when the war is over. I didn't know it, but the country beats the city all hollow."

She cast a loving glance round at the countryside, as if stirred by a revelation. Her life had been the gray slums, days spent in a factory, and the sordid compensation afforded by the cafés. Everything that went on here seemed to her as jolly as a picnic. She jumped down and ran to the village well. Probably she believed she was drinking at the very breast of mother earth.

"Have you done any fighting here?"

"No. The rebels kick up a little dust now and then, but . . . We see a truck load of men from time to time and hope that they will come along this road. But nothing has come by in two weeks."

They were awaiting their first enemy. In the rebel village opposite sat another half-dozen militiamen awaiting a first enemy. Twelve warriors alone in the world.

I have spent two days at the front traveling up and down country roads, and I have still to hear gunfire. I have seen nothing but endless little roads that have led us from vineyard to vineyard and from harvest to harvest. These things belong to another world, they are a part of a world of peace. In a flooded countryside, roads slope gently down and disappear under the water. The roads here have been like that for us—dead ends. The signposts around us read "Saragossa: 9 miles."

84

But like the legendary city of Ys, Saragossa lies asleep and inaccessible under the waves.

With better luck, obviously, we would have come to a zone where cannon were rumbling and commanders snapping out terse orders. It is simply that the commanders and the cannon and the troops are so few. Obviously we might have come upon masses of men on the march; there are crossroads on this front where men are fighting and killing each other. It is simply that between them and us there is so much space. Everywhere I have looked, the front has resembled a wide-open door.

The tacticians and the artillery and the troops all exist, but to me it has seemed that the real war is not being fought here.

The partridge is tracked down among the underbrush, the young girl is struck down before her brothers' eyes, but this, the fact of death, is not what horrifies me. When death is allied to life I find it almost beguiling. For example, I should like to think that in the convent below a day of death was also a day of rejoicing. But this monstrous disregard of man's humanity, this callous rationalization whereby human lives are added or subtracted—this I will have no part of.

Men have lost respect for each other. They have become soulless bailiffs who stride into the house and scatter a family's possessions to the four winds with no sense whatever that they have destroyed a kingdom. . . . Here in Spain we see committees who delegate to themselves the right to decree a purge on the basis of standards that then shift, and then shift

85

again, until the purge becomes nothing but a massacre. Or take that general who, with a clear conscience, ordered his Moroccan troops to cut down hapless crowds as if he were some prophet erasing a heresy. Here human beings are felled like trees in a forest.

In Spain, people are on the march, but the individual, that universe, calls in vain for help from the bottom of the mine.

Back to Barcelona this evening. Now I am sitting by the window in a friend's house. If I lean out, I can see a small cloister below. It's been bombed. The roof has fallen in, the walls are punctured by great gaping holes, and its most humble privacies lie there for all to see.

It makes me think of the anthills I used to disembowel in Paraguay; one blow of the pickax laid bare their innermost secrets. I suspect that the stalwarts who gutted this little shrine thought of it as a kind of anthill. One swift kick of a soldier's boot and all the little nuns tumbled out, and none of the passers-by who saw them scurrying about the ruins sensed that a tragedy had just happened.

But we are men, not ants, and the laws of number and space no longer apply. One scientist working in solitary absorption counterbalances in significance a whole city. The cancer patient roused from a fitful sleep is the focus of all human pain. A single miner may merit the death of a thousand men. When human beings are involved, statistics become a frightful game that I cannot play. People have said to me: "But what are a few dozen casualties compared to the whole population?"

"Does it matter that a few churches have burned down since the city has survived?" "Show me one sign of panic in Barcelona." These measurements I reject. The kingdom of man is not to be surveyed in this way.

The man who elects to closet himself in his cell or laboratory or love affair may seem to be standing a mere two steps from me, but actually he is immured in the solitary fastnesses of Tibet and the distance that lies between us I will never span. When I send the humble walls of the convent crashing into dust, I have no idea what civilization has vanished forever, like Atlantis plunging under the waves.

Each side is waiting for something to be born in the invisible. The rebels are waiting for the host of hesitant people in Madrid to declare themselves for Franco. Barcelona is waiting for Saragossa to waken out of an inspired dream, declare itself socialist, and fall. It is the thought more than the soldier that is besieging the town. The thought is the great hope and the great enemy. . . . The bombers, the shells, the militiamen under arms, by themselves have no power to conquer. On each side a single man entrenched behind his line of defense is better than a hundred besiegers. But thought might worm its way in.

From time to time there is an attack. From time to time the tree is shaken. Not to uproot it, but merely to see if the fruit is yet ripe. And if it is, a town falls.

5. Trigger-happy Fighters Are Indifferent to Human Life

BARCELONA. AUGUST 19.—Back from the front, I found friends in Barcelona who allowed me to join in their mysterious expeditions. We went deep into the mountains and were now in one of those villages that are possessed by a mixture of peace and terror.

"Oh, yes, we shot seventeen of them."

They had shot seventeen "fascists." The parish priest, the priest's housekeeper, the sexton, and fourteen village notables. Everything is relative, you see. When they read in their provincial newspaper the story of the life of [armaments manufacturer] Basil Zaharoff, master of the world, they transpose it into their own language. They recognize in him the nurseryman or the pharmacist. And when they shoot the pharmacist, in a way they are shooting Basil Zaharoff. The only one who does not understand is the pharmacist.

"Now we are all Loyalists together. Everything has calmed down."

88

Almost everything. The conscience of the village is tormented by one man whom I have seen at the tavern, smiling, helpful, so anxious to go on living! He comes to the pub in order to show us that, despite his few acres of vineyard, he too is part of the human race, suffers with rheumatism like it, mops his face like it with a blue handkerchief. He comes, and he plays billiards. Can one shoot a man who plays billiards? Besides, he plays badly with his great trembling hands. He is upset; he still does not know whether he is a fascist or not. He puts me in mind of those poor monkeys who dance before the boa constrictor in the hope of softening it.

There was nothing we could do for the man. For the time being we had another job in hand. Sitting on a table and swinging my legs at committee headquarters, while my companion, Pépin, pulled a bundle of soiled papers out of his pocket, I had a good look at these terrorists. Their looks belied their name. Honorable peasants with frank eyes and sober attentive faces, they were the same everywhere we went; and though we were foreigners possessing no authority, we were everywhere received with the same grave courtesy.

"Yes, here it is," said Pépin, a document in his hand. "His name is Laporte. Any of you know him?"

The paper went from hand to hand and the members of the committee shook their heads.

"No. Laporte? Never heard of him."

I started to explain something to them, but Pépin motioned me to be silent. "They won't talk," he said, "but they know him well enough."

89

Pépin spread his references before the chairman, saying casually: "I am a French socialist. Here is my party card."

The card was passed round and the chairman raised his eyes to us: "Laporte. I don't believe. . . ."

"Of course, you know him. A French monk. Probably in disguise. You captured him yesterday in the woods. Laporte, his name is. The French consulate wants him."

I sat swinging my legs. What a strange session! Here we were in a mountain village sixty miles from the French frontier, asking a revolutionary committee that shot even parish priests' housekeepers to surrender to us in good shape a French monk. Whatever happened to us, we would certainly have asked for it. Nevertheless, I felt safe. There was no treachery in these people. And why, as a matter of fact, should they bother to play tricks? We had absolutely no protection; we meant no more to them than Laporte; they could do anything they pleased.

Pépin nudged me. "I've an idea we have come too late," he said.

The chairman cleared his throat and made up his mind.

"This morning," he said, "we found a dead man on the road just outside the village. He must be there still."

And he pretended to send off for the dead man's papers.

"They've already shot him," Pépin said to me. "Too bad! They would certainly have turned him over to us. They are good kind people."

I looked straight into the eyes of these curious "good kind people." Strange: there was nothing in their eyes to upset me.

There seemed nothing to fear in their set jaws and the blank smoothness of their faces. Blank, as if vaguely bored. A rather terrible blankness. I wondered why, despite our unusual mission, we were not suspect to them. What difference had they established in their minds between us and the "fascist" in the neighboring tavern who was dancing his dance of death before the unavailing indifference of these judges? A crazy notion came into my head, forced upon my attention by all the power of my instinct: If one of those men yawned, I should be afraid. I should feel that all human communication had snapped between us.

After we left, I said to Pépin:

"This is the third village in which we have done this job, and I still cannot make up my mind whether the job is dangerous or not."

Pépin laughed and admitted that although he had saved dozens of men on these missions, he himself did not know the answer.

"Yesterday," he confessed, "I had a narrow squeak. I snaffled a Carthusian monk away from them just as they were about to shoot the fellow. The smell of blood was in the air, and . . . well, they growled a bit, you know."

I know the end of that story. Pépin, the socialist and notorious antichurch political worker, having staked his life to get that Carthusian, had hustled him into a motor car and there, by way of compensation, he sought to insult the priest by the finest bit of blasphemy he could summon: "You . . . you . . . you triple-damned monk!" he had finally sputtered.

91

This was Pépin's triumph. But the monk, who had not been listening, flung his arms around Pépin's neck and wept with happiness.

In another village they gave up a man to us. With a great air of mystery, four militiamen dug him up out of a cellar. He was a lively bright-eyed monk whose name I have already forgotten, disguised as a peasant and carrying a long gnarled stick scarred with notches.

"I kept track of the days," he explained. "Three weeks in the woods is a long time. Mushrooms are not specially nourishing, and they grabbed me when I came near a village."

The mayor of the village, to whom we owed this gift, was very proud of him.

"We shot at him a lot and thought we had killed him," he said. And then, by way of excuse for the bad marksmanship, he added: "I must say it was at night."

The monk laughed.

"I wasn't afraid."

We put him into the car, and before we threw in the clutch everybody had to shake hands all round with these terrible terrorists. The monk's hand was shaken hardest of all and he was repeatedly congratulated on being alive. To all these friendly sentiments he responded with a warmth of unquestionably sincere appreciation.

As for me, I wish I understood mankind.

We went over our lists. At Sitges lived a man who, we had been told, was in danger of being shot. We drove round and found his door wide open. Up a flight of stairs we ran into our skinny young man.

"It seems that these people are likely to shoot you," we told him. "Come back to Barcelona with us and you will be shipped home to France in the *Duquesne*."

The young man took a long time to think this over and then said:

"This is some trick of my sister's."

"What?"

"She lives in Barcelona. She would never pay for the child's keep and I always had to. . . ."

"Your family troubles are none of our affair. Are you in danger here, yes or no?"

"I don't know. I tell you, my sister. . . ."

"Do you want to get away, yes or no?"

"I really don't know. What do you think? In Barcelona, my sister . . ."

The man was carrying on his family quarrel through the revolution. He was going to stay here in order to do his sister in the eye.

"Do as you please," we said finally, and we left him where he was.

We stopped the car and got out. A volley of rifle shot had crackled in the still country air. From the top of the road we looked down upon a clump of trees out of which, a quarter of a mile away, stuck two tall chimneys. A squad of militiamen came up and loaded their guns. We asked what was going on.

They looked round, pointed to the chimneys, and decided that the firing must have come from the factory.

The shooting died down almost immediately, and silence fell again. The chimneys went on smoking peacefully. A ripple of wind ran over the grass. Nothing had changed visibly, and we ourselves were unchanged. Nevertheless, in that clump of trees someone had just died.

The silence now spoke louder than any rifle fire. If those guns had fallen quiet, it was because they no longer had a target.

A man, perhaps a whole family, had just slipped from one world into another. They were already vanishing under the green grass. Yet an evening breeze was stirring, plants continued to grow, the pale smoke curled upward. . . . Life goes on around the newly dead.

I know that death in itself is not tragic. Fresh green growing things flourished all around me, and I was reminded of a village in Provence I'd seen long ago thanks to a road detour. A few houses clustered around a steeple that was softly outlined against the evening sky. I stopped and sat down on the grass to savor this peace when the bell began to toll.

It was announcing to all the world that tomorrow an old woman, shriveled and worn, would be laid in earth, her work share done. The slow music mingling with the evening air seemed to me filled not with grief but with a tender, restrained happiness.

The bell was celebrating birth and death in a single voice. It announced the passing from one generation to the next. It was

94

telling the story of the human race. Over the body of the dead it celebrated life.

I felt only a great peace as I listened to the bell ring out the betrothal of the old woman and the earth. Tomorrow she would sleep under a royal blanket fashioned of flowers and singing cicadas.

One of the militiamen said that a girl had been killed at the factory, together with her brothers, but there was still some uncertainty about this. What excruciating simplicity! Our own peace of mind had not been invaded by those muffled sounds in the clump of greenery, by that brief partridge drive. The angelus, as it were, that had run out in that foliage had left us calm and unrepentant.

Human events display two faces, one of drama and the other of indifference. Everything changes according as the event concerns the individual or the species. In its migrations, in its imperious impulses, the species forgets its dead. This, perhaps, explains the unperturbed faces of these peasants. One feels that they have no special taste for horror; yet they will come back from that clump of trees on the one hand content to have administered their kind of justice, and on the other hand quite indifferent to the fate of the girl who stumbled against the root of the tree of death, who was caught by death's harpoon as she fled, and who now lies in the wood, her mouth filled with blood.

Here I touch the inescapable contradiction I shall never be able to resolve. For man's greatness does not reside merely in the destiny of the species: each individual is an empire. When

95

a mine caves in and closes over the head of a single miner, the life of the community is suspended.

His comrades, their women, their children, gather in anguish at the entrance to the mine, while below them the rescue party scratch with their picks at the bowels of the earth. What are they after? Are they consciously saving one unit of society? Are they freeing a human being as one might free a horse, after computing the work he is still capable of doing? Ten other miners may be killed in the attempted rescue: what inept cost accounting! Of course, it is not a matter of saving one ant out of a colony of ants! They are rescuing a consciousness, an empire whose significance is incommensurable with anything else.

Inside the narrow skull of the miner pinned beneath the fallen timber, there lives a world. Parents, friends, a home, the hot soup of evening, songs sung on feast days, loving kindness and anger, perhaps even a social consciousness and a great universal love, inhabit that skull. By what are we to measure the value of a man? His ancestor once drew a reindeer on the wall of a cave; and two hundred thousand years later that gesture still radiates. It stirs us, prolongs itself in us. Man's gestures are an eternal spring. Though we die for it, we shall bring up that miner from his shaft. Solitary he may be, universal he surely is.

V.

MADRID

1937

In June, 1937, Saint-Exupéry went to Spain as special correspondent for *Paris-Soir*. The following dispatches, which he wrote from Madrid and the Carabanchel front, appeared in *Paris-Soir* on June 27 and 28, and on July 3, 1937.

V. Madrid, 1937

Machine-gun bullets cracked against the stone above our heads as we skirted the moonlit wall. Low-lying lead thudded into the rubble of an embankment that rose on the other side of the road. Half a mile away a battle was in progress, the line of fire drawn in the shape of a horseshoe ahead of us and on our flanks.

Walking between wall and parapet on the white highway, my guide and I were able to disregard the spatter of missiles in a feeling of perfect security. We could sing, we could laugh, we could strike matches, without drawing upon ourselves the direct fire of the enemy. We went forward like peasants on their way to market. Half a mile away the iron hand of war would have set us inescapably upon the black chessboard of battle; but here, out of the game, ignored, the Republican lieutenant and I were as free as air.

Shells filled the night with absurd parabolas during their three seconds of freedom between release and exhaustion. There were the duds that dove without bursting into the ground; there were the travelers in space that whipped straight overhead, elongated in their race to the stars. And the leaden bullets that ricocheted in our faces and tinkled curiously in our ears were like bees, dangerous for the twinkling of an eye, poisonous but ephemeral.

Walking on, we reached a point where the embankment had collapsed.

"We might follow the cross-trench from here," my guide suggested. "But it's awfully dark. Maybe we'd do better to keep to the road."

I could sense his mocking smile. I wanted to know what war was like? He would see to it that I found out. The bullets that ricocheted and buzzed around me like insects had my fullest respect. I fancied that I could detect a purpose in their music. My body had become a magnet and it was the destiny of these bullets to seek it out. At the same time, I gave my guide his due. "He wants to rattle me, but he also wants to stay alive. Since he proposes our taking the road under this enchanted rain, it's because the road is relatively safe. He knows more about it than I."

"Let's stay on the road. It's a fine night!"

Obviously, I would have preferred to go on by the trench, but I was going to keep this to myself. I recognized his game from way back. I had played it myself at Cape Yubi. The "Danger—Off Bounds" signs were set up about twenty yards from the fort. Whenever an inspector came along who was a stuffed shirt and not too familiar with the desert, I would take him out for a little walk after dinner. While we chatted about this and that bit of airport business, I would be leading him straight out into the dunes. I waited for the diffident little remark that before long would repay me for miles of administrative red tape: "Uh . . . it's getting a little late, isn't it? . . . Should we be turning back?" Now it was I who was in charge and my man was solidly hooked. We were far enough from the fort so that he did not dare go back alone. My victim was chained to me, and I would meander happily on for another hour with the flimsiest excuses. But because it was fatigue he was complaining of, I would thoughtfully suggest that he sit down right there and wait for me. I would pick him up on my way back. He would pretend to hesitate, measuring the deceptive sands, and then say heartily, "Well, after all, I do enjoy a good walk. . . ."

"Good!" and on I strode, farther and farther from our refuge, regaling him with stories about the cruel customs of the Moorish tribes.

Tonight I was the "inspector," I was being marched along in chains, but I was determined I would duck my head every other second before I would let slip some vague but revealing remark about the charms of that cross-trench. So we crept along our little safety groove without either of us winning the round. Then events took a serious turn and our game of a sudden seemed childish.

Not that we were in the line of machine-gun fire, or that a roving searchlight was about to spot us. It was not as bad as that. There had simply been a rustling overhead; a sort of celestial gurgle had sounded. It meant no harm to us, but the lieutenant remarked suddenly, "That is meant for Madrid," and we went down into the trench.

The trench ran along the crest of a hill a little before reaching the suburb of Carabanchel. In the direction of Madrid a part of the parapet had crumbled and we could see the city in the gap, white, strangely white, under the full moon. Hardly a mile separated us from those tall structures dominated by the tower of the telephone building.

Madrid was asleep—or rather Madrid was feigning sleep. Not a light, not a sound. Like clockwork, every two minutes the funereal fracas that we were henceforth to hear roared forth and was dissolved in a dead silence. It seemed to waken no sound and no stirring in the city, but was swallowed up each time like a stone in water.

Suddenly in the place of Madrid I felt that I was staring at a face with closed eyes. The hard face of an obstinate virgin taking blow after blow without a moan. Once again there sounded overhead that gurgling in the stars of a newly uncorked bottle. One second, two seconds, five seconds went by. There was an explosion and I ducked involuntarily. There goes the whole town, I thought.

But Madrid was still there. Nothing had collapsed. Not an eye had blinked. Nothing was changed. The stone face was as pure as ever.

"Meant for Madrid," the lieutenant repeated mechanically. He taught me to tell these celestial shudders apart, to follow the course of these sharks rushing upon their prey:

"No, that is one of our batteries replying. . . . That's theirs, but firing somewhere else. . . . There's one meant for Madrid."

Waiting for an explosion is the longest passage of time I know. What things go on in that interminable moment! An enormous pressure rises, rises. Will that boiler ever make up its mind to burst? At last! For some that meant death, but there are others for whom it meant escape from death. Eight hundred thousand souls, less half a score of dead, have won a last-minute reprieve. Between the gurgling and the explosion eight hundred thousand lives were in danger of death.

Each shell in the air threatened them all. I could feel the city out there, tense, compact, a solid. I saw them all in the mind's eye—men, women, children, all that humble population crouching in the sheltering cloak of stone of a motionless virgin. Again I heard the ignoble crash and was gripped and sickened by the downward course of the torpedo. . . . Torpedo? I scarcely knew what I was saying. "They . . . they are torpedoing Madrid." And the lieutenant, standing there counting the shells, said:

"Meant for Madrid. Sixteen."

I crept out of the trench, lay flat on my stomach on the parapet, and stared. A new image has wiped out the old. Madrid with its chimney pots, its towers, its portholes, now looks like a ship on the high seas. Madrid all white on the black waters of the night. A city outlives its inhabitants. Madrid, loaded with emigrants, is ferrying them from one shore to the other of life. It has a generation on board. Slowly it navigates through the centuries. Men, women, children fill it from garrett to hold. Resigned or quaking with fear, they live only for the moment to come. A vessel loaded with humanity is being torpedoed. The purpose of the enemy is to sink Madrid as if she were a ship.

Stretched out on the parapet I do not care a curse for the rules of war. For justifications or for motives. I listen. I have learned to read the course of these gurglings among the stars. They pass quite close to Sagittarius. I have learned to count slowly up to five. And I listen. But what tree has been sundered by this lightning, what cathedral has been gutted, what poor child has just been stricken, I have no means of knowing.

This same afternoon I witnessed a bombardment in the town itself. All the force of this thunderclap had to burst on the Gran Via in order to uproot a human life. One single life. Passers-by had brushed rubbish off their clothes; others had scattered on the run; and when the light smoke had risen and cleared away, the betrothed, escaped by miracle without a scratch, found at his feet his *novia*, whose golden arm a moment before had been in his, changed into a blood-filled sponge, changed into a limp packet of flesh and rags.

He knelt down, still uncomprehending, and nodded his head slowly, as if saying to himself, "Something very strange has happened."

This marvel spattered on the pavement bore no resemblance to what had been his beloved. Misery was excruciatingly slow to engulf him in its tidal wave. For still another second, stunned by the feat of the invisible prestidigitator, he cast a bewildered glance round him in search of the slender form, as if it at least should have survived. Nothing was there but a packet of muck.

Gone was the feeble spark of humanity. And while in the man's throat there was brewing that shriek which I know not what deferred, he had the leisure to reflect that it was not those lips he had loved but their pout, not them but their smile. Not those eyes, but their glance. Not that breast, but its gentle swell. He was free to discover at last the source of the anguish love had been storing up for him, to learn that it was the unattainable he had been pursuing. What he had yearned to embrace was not the flesh but a downy spirit, a spark, the impalpable angel that inhabits the flesh.

I do not care a curse for the rules of war and the law of reprisal. Who was the first to begin? Retort calls forth retort always, and the first murderer among us has slipped away long since into the night of time. I distrust logic more than ever. Let the teacher demonstrate to me that fire does not burn flesh. I will thrust my hand into the fire and without benefit of logic I will know that somewhere his reasoning is false.

I have seen a young girl stripped of her gown of light. Am I to believe that reprisals are justified?

As for the military advantage of such a bombardment, I simply cannot grasp it. I have seen housewives disemboweled, children mutilated; I have seen the old itinerant market crone sponge from her treasures the brains with which they were spattered. I have seen a janitor's wife come out of her cellar and douse the sullied pavement with a bucket of water, and I am still unable to understand what part these humble slaughterhouse accidents play in warfare.

A moral role? But a bombardment turns against the bombarder! Each shell that fell upon Madrid fortified something in the town. It persuaded the hesitant neutral to plump for the defenders. A dead child weighs heavily in the balance when it is one's own. It was clear to me that a bombardment did not disperse—it unified. Horror causes men to clench their fists, and in horror men join together.

The lieutenant and I crawled along the parapet. Face or ship, Madrid stood erect, receiving blows without a moan. But men are like this; slowly but surely, ordeal fortifies their virtues.

Because of the ordeal my companion's heart was high. He was thinking of the hardening of Madrid's will. He stood up with his fists on his hips, breathing heavily. Pity for the women and the children had gone out of him.

"That makes sixty," he counted grimly.

The blow resounded on the anvil. A giant smith was forging Madrid.

We turned and walked on toward the outer lines of Carabanchel. Around us in a half circle the front quickened to a distant, incoherent fusillade that rolled across the sky like pebbles flung up and sucked back by the tide. At times the firing spread out twenty miles and more along the line like an epidemic, like the flames from firedamp. Then everything subsided, fell quiet, and withdrew into itself. It is in such moments of unbroken silence that you hear war dying.

All hatreds are relinquished, and one instant of such calm is enough to change the face of the world. There is no need to return a blow, no need to await a counterblow, no need to snatch up any challenge. This is the chance never to fire another shot, and the heart stops beating. Now let whoever shoots first bear the onus of war. To save the peace we need only sense this moment of silence. It is here, gentle as a shepherd. Here, asking us to listen. . . .

But then, before everyone has had the chance to hear, somewhere a gun cracks through the night air. Somewhere a flame leaps up from still live ashes. Somewhere war is revived by the act of a single murderer who is not responsible for his deed.

I was thinking of the silence that follows after something explodes, whether mine or bomb, when an eddy of dust enveloped us. I jumped, but the lieutenant strode on ahead of me and I read in his steady farmer's gait his refusal to concern himself with such outbursts. Habit? Scorn of death? Resignation? I was slowly learning that a man builds his war courage like a turtle its shell. Imagination is put forcibly to sleep. Anything happening more than thirty feet away is consigned to another universe. But I was still turning to look in the direction of the thunder, still trying to sort out the sounds.

The empty world was repopulated as we came up to the first-line trenches. The tips of cigarettes reddened here and there; the beam from a pocket flashlight sliced the darkness.

We slipped blindly along the line of trenches that wound past the small houses of Carabanchel. We were skirting, without being able to see it, a narrow street, the one barrier that separated us from the enemy. Several trenches turned away from it to burrow down into cellars. Here men slept, stood watch, fired through narrow loopholes. We mingled now with this strange submarine life. I brushed against the submerged figures of strangers. Now and then, my guide's hand gently pushed a mute shadow aside and shoved me into the lookout's place. The loophole was covered with a ragged cloth. I drew it back and peered outside. I saw nothing. Nothing except a wall opposite, and a strange lunar glow like light radiated through water. As I replaced the cloth, I felt as if I were mopping the moon's watery path.

Some message was being passed among the men, and I caught word that there would be a predawn attack. It was a matter of blowing up thirty houses in Carabanchel. Thirty among a hundred thousand concrete fortresses. There would be no artillery support; one by one, the houses would be breached with hand grenades and their gutted cells occupied. I thought of how you catch fish by dragging the hook along the crevices in a rock. I felt vaguely squeamish as I looked at these men who presently would take a gulping breath of air and plunge into the blue night, and who, if ever they reached the wall opposite, would hurl themselves into a mortal embrace under those rocks. How many would sink down before they had taken a dozen steps, drowned in the light of the moon?

Their expressions had not changed. They were waiting to do the job that must be done. All were volunteers here. Each man had renounced personal hopes and freedom to join the great muster. This was a routine attack. You dip into the human granary and at sowing time you scatter a handful of seed.

Fear began to show itself in a slight restlessness. Random shots became more frequent. The men feared the enemy as if they knew he had been alerted and was preparing God knows what desperate retaliation. They peered into the shadows, seeking him out. It was their own victim they feared, the savage reaction of the victim who feels the knife at his throat. These men were searching now for the silent enemy, the maniac at large in the countryside hatching violence, and they fired at silence. They believed they would draw his fire in reply. They feared phantoms, not other men. And it was a phantom who replied.

Then, there in the bottom of our hold, we heard our ship's timber begin to creak. Something was being slowly breached, and moonlight flowed in through the cracks. The men withstood this bodiless invasion of moon, night, and sea. Again and again the storm broke over us and we were shaken by the blows of a battering ram. Outside, the bullets that sucked up the breathable air made the men feel imprisoned, but the mines and mortars that were exploding now at quickened intervals unnerved them; each struck at them like the assault of a murderer, like a knife plunged into one's heart by a stranger.

Someone said, under his breath, "They're going to attack first, I bet."

The pressure from that last explosion struck us like a solid wave. The men quivered but did not move. I wished I understood what it was that held them magnetized like this. Tomorrow I would ask the sergeant beside me, if he came back alive. "Sergeant," I'd say, "why are you willing to die?"

The men did not move, but they shuddered like a tree under the blows of an ax. A man is attacked slowly, like a tree. He stands upright, but each added blow bites deeper and here in the night I could feel the boughs trembling.

Machine guns spouted rivers of sparks. The fire was becoming exasperated, the shots were no longer the fruit of individual decisions. Something was cracking the whole length of the trenches. I watched the machine gun nearest me veer from side to side, swinging its scythe two feet above the dark earth. Two feet above the dark earth nothing breathed. And yet something was moving out there. It was a ghost; the men were raging at a ghost they could not exorcise.

Were the others attacking? To me it all smacked of witchcraft. I'd seen nothing through that loophole, I would swear to it, nothing but a star. Yet beside me the machine gunner was loosing gust upon gust of shot, and the star trembled on the surface of the water. The night was composing a spell, men were contending with stars, and the watch who was slowly raising his arm was about to announce, announce. . . .

Everything seemed to explode at once. My thoughts were racing, pounding in my head. Like the others, I was thinking,

I don't want, I don't want. . . . As I crouch here, I don't want the night to toss the weight of a man's body on my shoulders. I don't want to hear an animal cry out beside me. I don't want them to harvest me today for the great stone tombs. Oh, for a gun! I strike out blindly. Watch out! I will hit anything that stirs one step forward. I move as one with the machine gunner, I make my fire pirouette in step with his. The stream of bullets is like the flourish of a saber. Watch out! I do not want to kill men, I want to kill the night, war, the horror, the pale phantom that, beyond the bounds of nightmare, moves one step nearer. . . .

Ouf! That was real panic.

We gathered around the captain. The sergeant was making a report. It had been a false alarm, but the enemy was evidently alerted. Should the attack proceed?

The captain shrugged. He, too, simply carried out orders. He pushed two glasses of brandy toward us.

"You go out first, with me," he said to the sergeant. "Have a drink and go get some sleep."

The sergeant drank and went off to sleep. Round the table a dozen of us were sitting up. All the chinks in this room were caulked up; not a trickle of light could escape; the glare within was so dazzling that I blinked. The brandy was sweet, faintly nauseating, and its taste was as mournful as a drizzle at daybreak. I was in a daze, and when I had drunk I shut my eyes and saw behind my lids those ruined and ghostly houses bathed in a greenish radiance as of moonglow under water, that I had stared at a few minutes before through the sentry's loophole. Someone on my right was telling a funny story. He was talking very fast and I understood about one word in three.

A man came in half drunk, reeling gently in this half-real world. He stood rubbing a stubble of beard and looking us over with vague affectionate eyes. His glance slid across to the bottle, avoided it, came back to it, and turned pleadingly to the captain.

The captain laughed softly, and the man, suddenly hopeful, laughed too. A light gust of laughter ran over the roomful of men. The captain put out his hand and moved the bottle noiselessly out of reach. The man's glance simulated despair, and a childish game began, a sort of mute ballet which, in the fog of cigarette smoke and the weariness of the watch with its anticipation of the coming attack, was utterly dreamlike. I sat hypnotized by this atmosphere of the slowly ending vigil, reading the hour in the stubbles of beard while out of doors a sealike pounding of cannon waxed in intensity.

Soon afterward these men were to scour themselves clean of their sweat, their brandy, the filth of their vigil, in the regal waters of the night of war. I felt in them something so near to spotless purity! Meanwhile, as long as it would last, they were dancing the ballet of the drunkard and the bottle. They were determined that this game should absorb them utterly. They were making life last as long as it possibly could. But there on the shelf stood a battered alarm clock, set to sound the zero hour. No one so much as glanced at it but me, and my glance was furtive. They would all hear it well enough, never fear! Its ringing would shatter the stifling air.

The clock would ring out. The men would rise to their feet and stretch themselves. They would be sure to make this gesture which is instinctive in every man about to tackle the problem of survival. They would stretch themselves, I say, and they would buckle on their harness. The captain would pull his revolver out of his holster. The drunk would sober up. And all these men, without undue haste, would file into the passage. They would go as far as that rectangle of pale light which is the sky at the end of the passage, and there they would mutter something simple like "Look at that moon!" or "What a night!" And then they would fling themselves into the stars.

Scarcely had the attack been called off by telephone, scarcely had these men, most of whom had been doomed to die in the attack upon that concrete wall, begun to feel themselves safe, begun to realize that they were certain of trampling their sweet planet in their rough clogs one more day, scarcely were their minds at peace, when all in chorus began to lament their fate.

"Do they think we are a lot of women?" "Is this a war or isn't it?" "A fine general staff!" they grumbled sarcastically. Can't make up its mind about anything. Wants to see Madrid bombarded and kids smashed to bits. Here they were, ready to rip up those enemy batteries and fling them over the backs of mountains to save innocence imperiled, and the staff tied them hand and foot, condemned them to inaction.

It was clear enough, and the men admitted it, that none of them might have come up again after their dive into the moonlight, and that they ought in reality to be very happy to be alive and able to grouse against G.H.Q. and go on drinking their consoling brandy—and, by the way, since the second telephone message, two curious things had happened; the brandy tasted better and the men were now drinking it cheerfully rather than moodily.

Yet at the same time I saw nothing in their vehemence that made me think it either silly or boastful. I could not but remember that all of them had been ready to die with simplicity.

What is more, I recognized in myself a like contradiction that did not disturb me at all. I was a mere spectator, of course. I did not share their reasons for facing risks, so that I, even more than they, had wished in the dark depths of my being that the certain disaster on which I was embarked would be called off. Nevertheless, now that a long day of rejoicing was assured me, now that I had nothing to fear, I also regretted some mysterious thing that was a part of that promised havoc.

Day broke. I scrubbed my face in the freezing water of the village pump. Coffee steamed in the bowls under an arbor forty yards from the enemy outpost, half-wrecked by the midnight firing but safe in the truce of dawn. Now freshly washed, the survivors gathered here to commune in life rather than in death, to share their white bread, their cigarettes, their smiles. They came in one by one, the captain, Sergeant R——, the lieutenant, and the rest, planted their elbows solidly on the table, and sat facing this treasure that they had been judicious enough to despise at a moment when it seemed it must be abandoned, but which had now recovered its price. "*Salud, amigo!*" they sang out as they clapped one another on the shoulder.

I loved the freezing wind that caressed us and the shining sun that warmed us beneath the touch of the wind. I loved the mountain air that was filling me with gladness. I rejoiced in the cheer of these men who sat in their shirtsleeves gathering fresh strength from their repast and making ready, once they had finished and risen to their feet, to knead the stuff of the world.

A ripe pod burst somewhere. From time to time a silly bullet spat against the stone wall. Death was abroad, of course, but wandering aimlessly and without ill intent. This was not death's hour. We in the arbor were celebrating life.

The captain was dividing the bread. I had known the urgency of hunger, but never before had I realized what dignity there is in the act of partaking of food. I had seen rations distributed by the truckload to hungry children, and that was a moving sight, but never before had I suspected the solemnity that inheres in sharing a meal. This whole platoon had risen up *de profundis*; and the captain sat breaking the white bread, that densely baked bread of Spain so rich in wheat, in order that each of his comrades, having stretched forth his hand, might receive a chunk as big as his fist and turn it into life.

These men had in truth risen *de profundis*. They were in very fact beginning a new life. I stared at them, and in particular at Sergeant R——, he who was to have been the first man out and who had gone to sleep in preparation for the attack. I was with them when they woke him up. Now Sergeant R—— had been well aware that he was to be the first man to step out into the line of fire of a machine-gun nest and dance in the moonlight that brief ballet at the end of which is death. His awakening had been the awakening of a prisoner in the death cell.

At Carabanchel the trenches wound among workmen's little houses whose furnishings were still in place. In one of these, a few yards from the enemy, Sergeant R—— was sleeping fully dressed on an iron cot. When we had lighted a candle and stuck it into the neck of a bottle, and had drawn forth out of the darkness that funereal bed, the first thing that came into view was a pair of clogs. Enormous clogs, iron-shod and studded with nails, the clogs of a sewer worker or a railway-track walker. All the poverty in the world was in those clogs. No man ever strode with happy steps through life in clogs like these; he boarded life like a longshoreman for whom life is a ship to be unloaded.

This man was shod in his tools, and his whole body was covered with the tools of his trade—cartridge belt, gun, leather harness. His neck was bent beneath the heavy collar of the draught horse. Deep in caves, in Morocco, you can see millstones worked by blind horses. Here in the ruddy wavering light of the candle we were waking up a blind horse and sending him out to the mill.

"Hi! Sergeant!"

He sent forth a sigh as heavy as a wave and turned slowly and massively over toward us so that we saw a face still asleep and filled with anguish. His eyes were shut, and his mouth, to which clung a bubble of air, was half open like the mouth of a drowned man. We sat down on his bed and watched his laborious awakening. The man was clinging like a crab to submarine depths, grasping in his fists I know not what dark seaweed. He opened and shut his hands, pulled up another deep sigh, and escaped from us suddenly with his face to the wall, obstinate with the stubbornness of an animal refusing to die, turning its back on the slaughterhouse.

"Hi! Sergeant!"

Once again he was drawn up from the bottom of the sea, swam toward us, and we saw again his face in the candlelight. This time we had hobbled our sleeper; he would not get away from us again. He blinked with closed eyes, moved his mouth round as if swallowing, ran his hand over his forehead, made one great effort to sink back into his happy dreams and reject our universe of dynamite, weariness, and glacial night, but it was too late. Something from without was too strong for him.

Thus the school bell invades the student's weary sleep. Desk, blackboard, penalties all are forgotten, and he dreams of a holiday, reveling in a country ramble, laughter. . . . He struggles to preserve this frail happiness as long as possible, he tries to plunge under the waves of sleep where no one can challenge his well-being, but the bell rings, rings, rings, inexorably calling him back to the injustice of man.

Sergeant R——— began to clothe himself in the weary flesh he had so recently shed, that flesh which in the chill of awakening was soon to know the old pains in the joints, the weight of the harness, and the stumbling race toward death. Not so much death as the discomfort of dying, the filth of the blood in which he would steep his hands when he tried to rise to his feet; the stickiness of that coagulating syrup. Not so much death as the Calvary of a punished child.

One by one he stretched his arms and then his legs, bringing up an elbow, straightening a knee, while his straps, his gun, his cartridge belt, the three grenades hanging from his belt, all hampered the final strokes of this swimmer in the sea of sleep. At last he opened his eyes, sat up on the bed, and stared at us, mumbling, "Huh! Oh! Are we off?"

And as he spoke, he simply stretched out his hand for his rifle.

"No," said the captain. "The attack has been called off."

Sergeant R———, let me tell you that we made you a present of your life. Just that. As much as if you had stood at the foot of the electric chair. And God knows, the world sheds ink enough on the pathos of pardon at the foot of the electric chair. We brought you your pardon *in extremis*. No question about it. In your mind there was nothing between you and death but a thickness of tissue paper. Therefore you must forgive me my curiosity. I stared at you, and I shall never forget your face. It was a face touching and ugly, with a humped nose a little too big, high cheekbones, and the spectacles of an intellectual. How does man receive the gift of life? I can answer that. A man sits still, pulls a bit of tobacco out of his pocket, nods his head slowly, looks up at the ceiling, and says:

"Suits me."

Then he nods his head again and adds: "If they'd sent us a couple of platoons the attack might have made sense. The lads would have pitched in. You'd have seen what they can do."

Sergeant, Sergeant, what will you do with this gift of life?

Now, Sergeant at peace, you are dipping your bread into your coffee. You are rolling cigarettes. You are like the lad who has been told he will not be punished after all. And yet, like the rest, you are ready to start out again tonight on that brief dash at the end of which the only thing a man can do is kneel down.

Over and over in my head there goes the question I have wanted to ask you ever since last night, "Sergeant, what is it that makes you willing to die?"

But I know that it is impossible to ask such a question. It would offend a modesty in you which you yourself do not know to be there, but which would never forgive me. You could not answer with high-sounding words; they would seem false to you and in truth they would be false. What language could be chaste enough for a modest man like you?

But I am determined to know, and I shall try to get round the difficulty. I shall ask you seemingly idle questions, and you will answer.

If I understood your answer, Sergeant, you hardly know yourself. You were a bookkeeper in Barcelona. You added up your columns of figures every day without worrying very much about the struggle against the rebels. But one of your friends joined up, and then a second friend; and you were disturbed to find yourself undergoing a curious transformation; little by little your columns of figures seemed to you futile. Your pleasures, your work, your dreams, all seemed to belong to another age.

But even that was not important, until one day you heard that one of your friends had been killed on the Málaga front. He was not a friend for whom you would ever have felt you had to lay down your life. Yet that bit of news swept over you, over your narrow little life, like a wind from the sea. And that morning another friend looked at you and said, "Do we or don't we?" And you said, "We do."

You never really wondered about the imperious call that compelled you to join up. You accepted a truth that you could never translate into words, but whose self-evidence overpowered you. And while I sat listening to your story, an image came into my mind, and I understood.

When the wild ducks or the wild geese migrate in their season, a strange tide rises in the territories over which they sweep. As if magnetized by the great triangular flight, the barnyard fowl leap a foot or two into the air and try to fly.

120

The call of the wild strikes them with the force of a harpoon and a vestige of savagery quickens their blood. All the ducks on the farm are transformed for an instant into migrant birds, and into those hard little heads, till now filled with humble images of pools and worms and barnyards, there swims a sense of continental expanse, of the breadth of seas and the salt taste of the ocean wind. The duck totters to right and left in its wire enclosure, gripped by a sudden passion to perform the impossible and by a sudden love whose object is a mystery.

Even so is man overwhelmed by a mysterious presentiment of truth, so that he discovers the vanity of his bookkeeping and the emptiness of his domestic felicities. But he can never put a name to this sovereign truth. Men explain these brusque vocations by the need to escape or the lure of danger—as if we knew where the need to escape and the lure of danger themselves came from. They talk about the call of duty—but what is it that makes the call of duty so pressing? What can you tell me, Sergeant, about that uneasiness that seeped in to disturb your peaceful existence?

The call that stirred you must torment all men. Whether we dub it sacrifice, or poetry, or adventure, it is always the same voice that calls. But domestic security has succeeded in crushing out that part in us that is capable of heeding the call. We scarcely quiver; we beat our wings once or twice and fall back into our barnyard.

We are prudent people. We are afraid to let go of our petty reality in order to grasp at a great shadow. But you, Sergeant, did discover the sordidness of those shopkeepers' bustlings, those petty pleasures, those petty needs. You felt that men did not live like this. And you agreed to heed the great call without bothering to try to understand it. The hour had come when you must molt, when you must rise into the sky.

The barnyard duck had no notion that his little head was big enough to contain oceans, continents, skies; but of a sudden here he was beating his wings, despising corn, despising worms, battling to become a wild duck.

There is a day of the year when the eels must go down to the Sargasso Sea, and come what may, no one can prevent them. On that day they spit upon their ease, their tranquillity, their tepid waters. Off they go over plowed fields, pricked by the hedges and skinned by stones, in search of the river that leads to the abyss.

Even so, did you feel yourself swept away by that inward migration about which no one had ever said a word to you? You were ready for a sort of bridal that was a mystery to you, but in which you had to participate. "Do we or don't we? We do." You went up to the front in a war that at bottom meant little to you. You took to the road as spontaneously as those silvery beings, shining in the fields on their way to the sea or that black triangle in the sky.

What were you after? Last night you almost reached your goal. What was it you discovered in yourself that was so ready to burst from its cocoon? At daybreak your comrades were full of complaint. Tell me, of what had they been defrauded? What had they discovered in themselves that was about to show itself, and that now they wept for?

I don't care to know whether or not they were afraid last night, whether or not they hoped the massacre would be called off, whether, even, they were poised to run. Because they did not run. They were prepared to begin all over again. Sometimes certain migratory birds set out over the ocean, flying into the wind. This widens the ocean so much for them that they cannot be sure of reaching the farther shore. But they carry in their little heads visions of sun and warm sands, and these sustain their flight.

What, Sergeant, were the visions that governed your destiny and justified your risking your life in this adventure? Your life, your only treasure! We have to live a long time before we become men. Very slowly do we plait the braid of friendships and affections. We learn slowly. We compose our creation slowly. And if we die too early we are in a sense cheated out of our share. We have to live a long time to fulfill ourselves.

But you, by the grace of an ordeal in the night which stripped you of all that was not intrinsic, you discovered a mysterious creature born of yourself. Great was this creature, and never shall you forget him. And he is yourself. You have had the sudden sense of fulfilling yourself in the instant of discovery, and you have learned suddenly that the future is now less necessary for the accumulation of treasures. That creature within you who opened his wings is not bound by ties to perishable things; he agrees to die for all men, to be swallowed up in something universal.

A great wind swept through you and delivered from the matrix the sleeping prince you sheltered—Man within you.

You are the equal of the musician composing his music, of the physicist extending the frontier of knowledge, of all those who build the highways over which we march to deliverance. Now you are free to gamble with death. What have you now to lose?

Let us say you were happy in Barcelona; nothing more can ruin that happiness. You have reached an altitude where all loves are of the same stuff. Perhaps you suffered on earth, felt yourself alone on the planet, knew no refuge to which you might fly? What of that! Sergeant, this day you have been welcomed home by love.

VI.

PEACE OR WAR?

The following three articles were commissioned by *Paris-Soir* in the aftermath of Munich and were published on October 2, 3, and 4, 1938.

1. Needed: A Language for Speaking the Truth

We are living through deeply anxious days, and if we are to relieve our anxiety we must diagnose its causes. We have elected to save the peace. To save the peace, we have had to do violence to friends. There is no question but that many of us were ready to risk our lives to meet the obligations of friendship. Such people now feel a kind of shame. Had they sacrificed the peace instead, they would also have felt ashamed. For then they would have sacrificed man; they would have given their consent to the irreparable destruction of the cathedrals and libraries and laboratories of Europe; they would have given their consent to the annihilation of her traditions and the transformation of the world into a cloud of ashes. Why else have we wavered, now this way, now that? When we thought peace was threatened, we discovered the abomination of war. When we thought war had been averted, we tasted the odium of peace.

We must not indulge in self-abasement, for neither decision

127

would have spared us this shame. We must rather collect ourselves and seek for the meaning of our disgust. When men are caught in such a profound conflict, it is because they have not seen the problem clearly. When the physicist discovered that as the earth revolves it draws in its wake the ether through which light travels, and discovered at the same time that the ether itself is motionless, he did not abandon science. He corrected his language and abandoned his notion of the ether.

If we are to discover the sources of our anxiety, we probably have to rise above recent events. For the moment, we must forget the Sudetenland. We become blind when we look at things from too near. We must think about war, since we at once accept and reject it.

I shall be criticized, I know, for what I am about to write. Newspaper readers want hard facts, not opinions. Opinions belong in magazines or books. I disagree with this.

In my mind's eye I can still see the first night flight I made in Argentina. It was pitch-dark. Yet in the black void, I could see the lights of man shining down below on the plain, like faintly luminous earthbound stars. Each star was a beacon signaling the presence of a human mind. Here a man was meditating on human happiness, perhaps, or on justice or peace. Lost among this flock of stars was the star of some solitary shepherd. There, perhaps, a man was in communication with the heavens, as he labored over his calculations of the nebula of Andromeda. And there, a pair of lovers. These fires were burning all over the countryside, and each of them, even the most humble, had to be fed. The fire of the poet, of the teacher, of the carpenter. But among all these living fires, how many closed windows there were, how many dead stars, fires that gave off no light for lack of nourishment.

Let the journalist be wrong in his opinions; it does not matter, no one is infallible. Suppose he does not enter each and every one of those dwellings. This does not matter. It is the homes where men keep vigil that endow a country with its meaning. The journalist does not know which among them will commune with him. That also does not matter. He hopes simply to provide kindling that will help feed such fires scattered here and there over the face of the earth.

Those days we spent crowding around the loudspeakers were hard. It was rather like queuing up outside the factory gate for jobs to be handed out. Men turned out in droves to listen to Hitler, and they could already see themselves being herded into freight cars and shipped off to man the glistening steel machines in the factory that war today has become. They behaved as if they had already been impressed into some gigantic slave gang: the truth-seeker abandoned the calculations that enabled him to speak with the stars; the father rose abruptly and left the evening meal that nourished hearts no less than bodies; the gardener turned away from his rose. We were already uprooted, disoriented, and hurled pell-mell into the millrace.

We did not act this way out of any spirit of sacrifice; we were abandoning ourselves to the absurd. We were drowned in contradictions we could no longer resolve and discouraged by the incoherence of events no language could clarify. We were ready to accept the bloody tragedy blindly because the duties it would lay upon us would be simple duties.

We did realize that any war, since war is now waged with benefit of bombs and mustard gas, could result only in the destruction of Europe. However, people are much less sensitive to descriptions of catastrophe than we often suppose. Week after week, in the upholstered comfort of our movie houses we witnessed bombardments in Spain and China. We heard explosions that were shaking whole cities to their foundations, and we remained untouched. We stared half-admiringly at the twisting fringes of soot and ashes that these volcanic lands spiraled slowly toward the sky. And yet! And yet! It was grain from the granaries, it was the heritage of generations, the charred flesh of children which was being squandered in that smoke, which was slowly fattening that black cloud!

I have walked along the bombed streets of Arguelez, in Madrid, where, like pierced eyeballs, windows framed only a milky blob of sky. Only the walls had survived; behind those ghostly façades the contents of six stories lay reduced to a few yards of rubble. For generations, massive oak beams had supported the building of family histories, composed as always out of the commonplace: here, when the thunder began to rumble, a servant had drawn white curtains together; here a mother's cool hand had soothed the feverish head of a sick child; here a father had mulled over tomorrow's business deal.

These were foundations everyone thought eternal, yet one explosion in the heart of night set them swaying until, like so many scuttles, they tipped their burden into the foundry furnace.

However, the impact of these horrors does not carry from screen to spectator. We watch indifferently as the bomber's load plummets noiselessly earthward to gut these living habitations.

I do not want to lapse into shrill indignation, because the real problem here is that we lack the key to understanding, which is an adequate language. We unmoved spectators are at the same time people who would risk our lives for a buried miner or for a child in distress. And simply to shudder at the havoc we witness proves nothing. I put no great trust in the efficacy of simple animal responses. Think of the surgeon as he makes his hospital rounds; he cannot respond like some tenderhearted girl to the sight of suffering. His compassion is too austere to be expended on the ulcer that, for him, is something he must cure. He palps the ulcer and does not hear the whimper of pain.

So it is in the hour of childbirth. When the groans begin, great excitement grips the household. Steps hurry in through the front door, fresh cloths are laid out, voices call back and forth, and no one is dismayed by screams that the young mother herself will forget, that will become encysted in memory, for they do not matter. Yet now she writhes and bleeds in pain. Gnarled arms support her; butcher's arms assist in the expulsion of the fruit, wrench flesh from flesh. But

131

everyone is busy, everyone is smiling. "Everything is going well," they whisper. They prepare a cradle; they prepare a warm bath; and suddenly they run toward the door, fling it wide, and cry, "Praise God, it's a boy!"

If we merely recite the horrors of war, we will never prevail against war. Neither will we prevail if we are content merely to hymn the sweetness of life and the cruelty of sterile widowhood. We have been talking about mothers' tears for thousands of years, yet it must be conceded that fine words have not prevented sons from dying.

Nor will we find salvation in rationalizations. So and so many dead, more or less. . . . What number may we deem acceptable? We will never establish peace on the basis of such wretched arithmetic. . . . We talk about "necessary sacrifices" or speak of "the grandeur and tragedy of war." Or, we may say nothing at all. Actually, we possess no language that enables us to sort the various kinds of death into categories unless we resort to complicated rationalizations. And both instinct and experience make us distrust this; everything, we have learned, can be proved. A truth does not prove; it clarifies.

Our present dilemma is as old as the human race; it has presided over every step of man's progress. Society is constantly evolving, and men have always had to struggle to understand current realities by means of a language that is outdated. We are prisoners of language and of the frozen metaphors it sweeps along in its wake. It is inadequate language that gradually becomes contradictory; the realities never become so. Man is freed only by the act of forging fresh concepts. Simply to imagine what the world of the future will be is not a sufficient action making for progress. How can we take into account unforeseen contradictions that will be born tomorrow of today's assumptions? They will require new syntheses, and thus will alter the course of history. The world of the future defies analysis. Man progresses when he forges the language in which he can formulate his concepts of the world of his own day. Newton did not prepare for the discovery of X-rays by foreseeing X-rays. Newton devised a simple language in order to describe phenomena known to him. And from this X-rays emerged. It is utopian to suppose any other method will work.

Do not search for ways and means whereby mankind can be saved from war. Rather ask yourself, "Why is it that we make war when we realize that it is monstrous and senseless? How is such a contradiction possible? What is the basis of it? What in the nature of war is so imperious that it can prevail over our horror and our fear of death?" If we can discover the answer to this, then and only then will we be able to avoid delivering ourselves helplessly into the power of a sightless destiny. Then and only then will we be saved from war.

Of course, you can retort by saying that the risk of war resides in man's irrationality. But by saying this, you disclaim man's ability to understand. You might as well assert that the earth revolves around the sun because such is God's will. Perhaps this is so. But into what equations can this will of God's be translated? Into what clear language can we translate our irrational susceptibility to war and thereby deliver ourselves of it?

The familiar explanations of savage instincts, greed, blood lust also seem inadequate keys to the dilemma. They overlook what may be truly essential. They ignore the asceticism that surrounds war. They ignore the sacrifice of life, the discipline, the brotherhood in the face of danger. They fail to take into account everything we find remarkable in men—in all men—who go to war and who, in so doing, tacitly accept privation and death.

Last year I visited the Madrid front, and I realized then how much more meaningful it is to come into direct contact with the realities of war than any amount of reading can be. The soldier is the only person who can teach us about war.

If we want to come to grips with what is universal in war, we must forget such things as opposing camps and we must avoid arguing over ideologies. Language bears within it such insoluble contradictions that one despairs of its contributing to man's salvation. For example, Franco bombs Barcelona, he says, because Barcelona massacred some monks. Ergo, by bombing Barcelona, Franco is defending Christian values. In the name of these Christian values, women and children in Barcelona are put to the torch. What, I ask you, is the Christian witness to make of this? You will tell me that these are the sad necessities of war. I say war is senseless. Absurd. One has to choose one's camp, yes. But I think it absurd that language compels men to contradict themselves.

Do not insist that your beliefs are evidence of the truth, for in that case, is not each of us right? The man who blames all the world's ills on hunchbacks is right. Let us, then, declare war on hunchbacks. Let us conjure up the image of a race of inimical hunchbacks. You will see how quickly our spirits will soar. And let us arraign these hunchbacks and confront them with the sum of obscenities, crimes, and lies of which they are guilty. This will be simple justice. And as we hang some poor innocent hunchback by the neck, we will shrug regretfully: "The horror of war, you see. . . . He is paying for the others. . . . He is paying for the crimes of the hunchbacks. . . ." And it is undeniable that hunchbacks, too, commit crimes.

We must put aside the passions and beliefs that divide us, for once we give them our allegiance, they bring in their wake a veritable Koran of unshakable truths and all the fanaticism that springs from them. It is possible to align men as men of the Right and men of the Left, as hunchbacks and non-hunchbacks, as fascists and as democrats; these distinctions are unassailable. But truth—and this we know—truth is what clarifies and not that which creates chaos.

What would we learn if we were to put a question to a man of war, whoever he may be, and if then, instead of listening to him struggle to answer in his poor, inadequate language, we were to watch him live his life and thereby tell us the meaning of his deepest hopes?

2. Enemy Voices in the Night Speak Across No Man's Land

On the Guadalajara front I sat at night in a dugout with a Republican squad made up of a lieutenant, a sergeant, and three men. They were about to go out on patrol duty. One of them (the night was cold) stood half in shadow with his head not quite through the neck of a sweater he was pulling on, his arms caught in the sleeves and waving slowly and awkwardly in the air like the short arms of a bear. Smothered curses, stubbles of beard, distant muffled explosions—the atmosphere was a strange compound of sleep, waking, and death. I thought of tramps on the road bestirring themselves, raising themselves up off the ground on heavy sticks. Caught in the earth, painted by the earth, their hands grubby with their gardenless gardening, these men were raising themselves painfully out of the mud in order to emerge under the stars. In these blocks of caked clay I could sense the awakening of consciousness, and as I looked at them I said to myself that across the way, at this very moment, the enemy was getting

into his harness, was thickening his body with woolen sweat-
ers; earth-crusted, he was breaking out of his mold of hardened mud. Across the way the same clay shaping the same
beings was wakening in the same way into consciousness.

Across the way, Lieutenant, slowly struggling to his feet is
a man who is your double, and who presently will die by
your hand. He also has renounced everything to serve the
cause he believes in. But what he believes in you believe in,
too, for who would consent to risk death except for truth,
justice, and love of his fellow men?

"They've been misled—I mean, the men opposite have been
misled," you'll tell me. But I have no use for politicians,
profiteers, and armchair experts, no matter which side they
belong to. They are the men who pull the strings, use the big
words, and fancy themselves leaders of men. The rest of us
they consider simpletons. But if their big words do take root,
it is because, like seeds borne by the winds to some distant
land, they fall upon a rich soil prepared to bear the burden of
the harvest.

The patrol moved forward across fields through crackling
stubble, knocking its toes against unseen rocks in the dark.
We were making our way down into a narrow valley on the
other side of which the enemy was entrenched. Caught in the
crossfire of artillery, the peasants had evacuated this valley,
and their deserted village lay here drowned in the waters of
war. Only their dogs remained, ghostly creatures that hunted

their pitiful prey in the day and howled in the night. At four in the morning, when the moon rose white as a picked bone, a whole village bayed at the dead divinity.

"Go down and find out if the enemy is hiding in that village," the commanding officer had ordered. Very likely on the other side the same order had been given.

We were accompanied by a sort of political agent, a civilian. "You'll hear them," he told me. "When we get nearer, we'll call out to the enemy. They're just across the valley, on that hill. Sometimes they answer."

I have forgotten his name, though not what he looked like. It seems to me he must have been rheumatic, and I remember that he leaned heavily on a knotted stick as we tramped forward in the night. His face was the face of a conscientious and elderly workman. I would have sworn that he was above politics and parties, above ideological rivalries. "Pity it is," he would say, "that as things are we cannot explain our point of view to the other fellow." He walked weighed down by his doctrine, like an evangelist. Across the way, meanwhile, was the other evangelist, a believer just as enlightened as this one, his boots just as muddy, his duty taking him on exactly the same errand.

We were moving steadily forward toward the lip of land that dominated the valley, toward that farthermost promontory, that ultimate terrace, toward the question we would call out to the enemy, as if we were questioning ourselves.

The night arched above us like a cathedral. No rifle shattered the silence. A truce? No, no, not that. It was more the feeling of a presence. One was listening for the two adversaries to speak forth in a single voice. Fraternization? Definitely not, if this means the weariness that fragments a front line into individuals and moves men to share their cigarettes and mingle with each other out of their sense of a common loss of human status.

Try making a gesture toward the enemy. It will lead to a kind of fraternization, perhaps, but at a level that engages an inarticulate segment of the mind and will not save us here below from carnage. For still we do not command the language to express what it is that unites us.

I felt I understood this agent who was accompanying us. Where did he come from, this man who kept his face set so steadily ahead? First, he and the peasants he grew up with had watched the land and learned how it lives. Surely he had walked long years behind a plow. Then he left village for factory, and he watched how men live. "Metallurgist . . . been a metallurgist for twenty years."

I have never heard a man speak about himself with such noble freedom and directness. "No schooling for me, though, . . . And teaching myself was hard, hard. . . . Tools, you see, I knew about. I knew how to use them, talk about them. I understood tools. . . . But when I wanted to think about things, about ideas and life, or if I wanted to talk to someone about such things. . . . You people, you see, are used to thinking abstractly. From the time you're children, they teach you how to find your way through those mazes of words that are all so full of contradictions. You don't remember, you can't even imagine any more how hard it is to reason. . . . But I worked at it, I kept at it. And little by little I began to limber up. I could feel it. Oh, don't think I don't know my limitations. . . . I'm a bumpkin still. I haven't ever learned about courtesy, for example, and manners bespeak the man, you know. . . ."

As I was listening to him, I remembered an impromptu school I'd come across one day, quite near the front. It had been set up in the shelter of a few rocks. A corporal was giving a lesson in botany. He was separating the petals of a wild poppy, initiating his pupils into one of the more gentle mysteries of nature. Old and hardened by life as they were, the men were almost childishly anxious as they struggled to understand. They had been told: "You're like brutes who've scarcely crawled out of your caves. You've got to join the civilized race." And they were hastening on, in their heavy, clumsy boots, to catch up.

What I had witnessed that day was the mind's awakening, and it was very like the rising of sap. Born out of clay, in the shadows of prehistory, the mind has ascended step by step to the peaks of a Descartes, Bach, or Pascal. And I was moved now as I listened to this man talk about the effort of thinking, of the impulse to grow. This is the way a tree grows. The mystery of life lies here. Life alone draws its stocks from the soil and against the drag of gravity raises them skyward.

How well I remember that cathedral night. The spirit of man sallying forth with bow and arrow. . . . The enemy to whom presently we would be calling. . . . And we ourselves, a caravan of pilgrims plodding over a black, crackling earth seeded with stars.

We do not know it, but we are in search of a gospel that will embrace all our provisional gospels. They spill too much human blood. We are marching toward a stormy Sinai.

And we have arrived. We stumble over a dazed sentinel, half asleep in the shelter of a low stone wall.

"Yes, here they sometimes answer. . . . Other times they call to us. . . . But sometimes they don't answer. It depends on how they feel."

Just like the gods.

The winding front-line trenches lie about a hundred yards behind us. Here the low breastworks shield a man only up to his chest; they serve as lookouts at night and during the day are abandoned. They face directly out over the abyss. We feel as if we are propping our elbows on a railing or parapet that has been flung out above the unknown, above the void.

I strike a match, intending to light a cigarette, and two powerful hands duck my head. Everybody has ducked, and I hear the whistle of bullets in the air. Then silence. The shots were fired high and the volley was not repeated, a mere reminder from the enemy of what constitutes decorum here. One does not light a cigarette in the face of the enemy.

We are joined by three or four men, wrapped in blankets, who had been posted behind neighboring walls.

"Looks as if the lads across the way were awake," one of them remarks.

"Do you think they'll talk tonight? We'd like to talk to them."

"One of them, Antonio, he talks sometimes."

"Call him."

The man in the blanket straightens up, cups his hands round his mouth, takes a deep breath, and calls out slowly and loudly: "An . . . to . . . ni . . . o!"

The call swells, unfurls, floats across the valley and echoes back.

"Better duck," my neighbor advises. "Sometimes when you call them, they let fly."

Crouched behind the stone wall, we listen. No sound of a shot. Yet we cannot say we have heard nothing at all, for the whole night is singing like a seashell.

"Hi! Antonio . . . o! Are you . . . ?"

The man in the blanket draws another deep breath and goes on:

"Are you asleep?"

"Asleep?" says the echo. "Asleep?" the valley asks. "Asleep?" the whole night wants to know. The sound fills all space. We scramble to our feet and stand erect in perfect confidence. They have not touched their guns.

I stand imagining them on their side of the valley as they listen, hear, receive this human voice, this voice that obviously has not stirred them to anger since no finger has pressed a trigger. True, they do not answer, they are silent; but how attentive must be that silent audience from which, a moment ago, a match had sufficed to draw a volley. Borne on the breeze of a human voice, invisible seeds are fertilizing that black earth across the valley. Those men thirst for our words as we for theirs. But their fingers, meanwhile, are on their triggers. They put me in mind of those wild things we would try in the desert to tame and that would stare at us, eat the food and drink the water we set out for them, and would spring at our throats when we made a move to stroke them.

We squatted well down behind the wall and held up a lighted match above it. Three bullets passed overhead. To the match they said, "You are forgetting that we are at war." To us, "We are listening, nevertheless. We can still love, though we stick to our rules."

Another giant peasant rested his gun against the wall, stood up, drew a deep breath, and let go:

"Antonio . . . o! It's me! Leo!"

The sound moved across the valley like a ship new-launched. Eight hundred yards to the far shore, eight hundred back—sixteen hundred yards. If they answered, there would be five seconds of time between our questions and their replies. Five seconds of silence, in which all war would be suspended, would go by between each question and each answer. Like an embassy on a journey, each time. What this meant was that even if they answered, we should still feel ourselves separated from them. Between them and us the inertia of an invisible world would still be there to be stirred into action. For the considerable space of five seconds we should be like men shipwrecked and fearful lest the rescue party had not heard their cries.

". . . ooo!"

A distant voice like a feeble wave has curled up to die on our shore. The phrase, the word, was lost on the way and the result is an undecipherable message. Yet it strikes me like a blow. In this impenetrable darkness a sudden flash of light has gleamed. All of us are shaken by a ridiculous hope. Something has made known to us its existence. We can be sure now that there are men across the way. It is as if in invisibility a crack had opened, as if. . . . Imagine a house at night, dark and its doors all locked. You, sitting in its darkness, feel a breath of cold air on your face. A single breath. What a presence!

Have you ever leaned over an abyss? I remember the fault at Chézery; it was a black fissure lost in the woods, perhaps four or five feet wide and ninety feet long. Not amounting to much, that is. I used to lie flat on my belly on the pine needles and let a stone slip from my hand down the smooth side of the crevice. No reply. One, two, three seconds passed and after that eternity I would finally hear a faint rumble, all the more stirring to me for its being so slow and so slight. Then the abyss seemed to me bottomless. And so it was that now a delayed echo created a whole world. The enemy, we, life, death, the war—all were contained and expressed in a few seconds of silence.

Again our signal is released, our ship sent forth, our caravan despatched into the desert, and we wait. They no doubt are preparing to receive that voice which strikes like a bullet to the heart.

There it comes again! ". . . time . . . sleep!"

Torn, mutilated as a truly urgent message must be, washed by the waves and soaked in brine, here is our message. The men who fired at our cigarettes have blown up their chests with air in order to send us this motherly bit of advice:

"Quiet! Go to bed! Time to sleep!"

It excites us. You who read this will perhaps think that these men were merely playing a game. In a sense they were. I am sure that, being simple men, if you had caught them at their sport they would have denied that it was serious. But games cover something deep and intense, else there would be no excitement in them, no pleasure, no power to stir us.

The game we perhaps thought we were only playing was too well attuned to the vaulted night, the march toward Sinai; it made our hearts beat too wildly for it not to be the answer to some real if undefined need within us. We exulted because communication had been re-established. Thus the scientist's hand trembles as the crucial experiment proceeds and he prepares to weigh the molecule. He will be noting one constant among a hundred thousand variables, and it might seem as if he were merely adding one grain of sand to the towers of science. Yet his heart pounds, for it is not a matter of a grain of sand. He holds a thread. He holds in his hand the thread by which knowledge of the universe is gathered in, for all things are interconnected. The rescue team trembles in the same way when they have cast their rope once, twice, twenty times, and feel at last the almost imperceptible tug telling them that the shipwrecked crew has grasped it. A tiny huddle of men had been lost among the fog-shrouded reefs, cut off from the world. And now the magic of a thread of cable links them to the men and women safely in port everywhere. Here we threw a fragile bridge out into the night, toward the unknown, and now it links the two sides of the world. It was as if we were marrying our enemy before dying by his hand.

But so slight, so fragile was the pontoon flung between our two shores that a question too awkward, a phrase too clumsy, would certainly upset it. Words lose themselves: only essential words, only the truth of truths would leave this frail bridge whole. And I can see him now, that peasant who stirred Antonio to speech and thus made himself our pilot, our ambassador; I can see him as he stood erect, as he rested his strong hands on the low stone wall and sent forth from his great chest that question of questions:

"Antonio! What are you fighting for?"

Let me say again that he and Antonio would be ashamed to think that you took them seriously. They would insist that it was all in fun. Later they would actually believe this, when they groped for words to describe what had moved them to do this thing and did not find them because in our meager language such words do not exist. Yet they had acted on the impulse of a being that lives within all of us and that someday with a mighty effort we will deliver. But I was there as that soldier stood waiting, and I know that his whole soul gaped wide to receive the answer. Here is the truncated message, the secret mutilated by five seconds of travel across the valley as an inscription in stone is defaced by the passing of the centuries:

". . . Spain!"

And then I heard:

". . . You?"

He got his answer. I heard the great reply as it was flung forth into space:

"The bread of our brothers."

And then the amazing:

"Good night, friend!"

And the response from the other side of the world:

"Good night, friend!"

And silence.

Probably they on the other side had, like us, snatched only a few ragged words. Such was the fruit of an hour's hard and dangerous march. These few words, echoes oscillating from hill to hill under the silent stars: "Spain" . . . "bread of our brothers."

And then, the hour having come, our patrol resumed its march. We began the descent toward the village that had been appointed for our rendezvous. On the other side, the same patrol, governed by the same necessities, was plunging into the same abyss. Under the guise of different words, both had proclaimed the same truths, yet this was not to preclude their dying together.

147

3. We Must Give Meaning to Men's Lives

The words we use contradict each other, but our aspirations are the same: the dignity of man, the bread of our brothers. We disagree not over objectives but over ways and means, which are the fruit of our varied reasoning. When we go off to war, intent on killing each other, we all march toward the same promised land.

We are only able to recognize this if we look at ourselves from a certain perspective. Then we perceive that really we are at war with ourselves. Our struggles, quarrels, and recriminations are the spasms of a single body torn by the pangs of childbirth. Something will be born of the travail, and it will eclipse the conflicts out of which it is engendered, but we shall have to make haste to forge the synthesis. We must assist in the delivery, else the creature will be stillborn.

We must never forget that modern warfare traffics in the bomb and in mustard gas. War is no longer delegated to a

148

group that garners heroes' laurels along the national frontier (and in so doing, I must admit, at a more or less heavy price enriches the spiritual patrimony of a people). War today is a kind of surgery; like insects, we locate the adversary's ganglia and administer the paralyzing sting.

Let war be declared, and the next instant our stations, bridges, and factories will be pulverized. Our asphyxiated cities will retch and spew their populations out over the countryside. Europe is an organism of two hundred million men. In the first moment of war, it will lose its entire nervous system, exactly as if it were burned out by acid; its control centers, regulatory glands, and semicircular canals will be one enormous cancer that will commence at once to corrode the whole. And how are two hundred million men to be fed? Grub as they will, they will never find roots enough.

When our contradictions become so intense, we must hasten to surmount them, for nothing can suppress a need that urgently demands recognition. Suppose the need finds its expression in a militaristic ideology. Make no mistake about it: in that case, we will go to war. We have indeed better ways than war to satisfy the needs that torment mankind, but it is futile to deny that the needs exist.

I once knew a South Moroccan officer whose name I will not mention for fear of embarrassing him. It would be instructive if we were to try to urge on him our reasons for hating war. If we did not convince him, should we dismiss him as a barbarian? First listen to this story.

During the war in the Rif, this officer was in command of

149

an outpost set down between two mountains filled with enemy tribesmen. One day, down from the mountain to the west came a group seeking a parley. Arabs and Frenchmen were talking over their tea when of a sudden a volley rang out. The tribesmen from the other mountain were charging the post. When the commandant sought to dismiss his guests before fighting off their allies, they said to him: "Today we are your guests. God will not allow us to desert you." They fought beside his men, saved the post, and then climbed back into their aerie.

But on the eve of the day when their turn had come to pounce upon the post they sent again to the commandant.

"We came to your aid the other day," their chief said.

"True."

"We used up three hundred of our cartridges for you."

"Very likely."

"It would be only just that you replace them for us."

The commandant was an officer and a gentleman. They were given their cartridges.

Truth for any man is that which makes him a man. A man who has fraternized with men on this high plane, who has displayed this sportsmanship and has seen the rules of the game so nobly observed on both sides in matters of life and death, is obviously not to be mentioned in the same breath with the shabby hearty demagogue who would have expressed his fraternity with the Arabs by a great clap on the shoulders and a spate of flattering words that would have humiliated them. You might argue with the captain that all was fair in war, but if you did he would feel a certain pitying contempt for you. And he would be right.

Do not try to explain to a Mermoz who is plunging toward the Chilean face of the Andes with victory in his heart that he's mistaken, that no letter—a merchant's perhaps—is worth his risking his life to deliver. Mermoz will laugh at you. Truth is the man that is born in him as he passes over the Andes.

And if the German today is ready to give his life for Hitler, you must understand that it is futile to argue with him about Hitler. The German finds in Hitler the opportunity to care intensely, to devote himself to a cause; because of Hitler, everything seems to him enlarged. We must understand that the power of any movement derives from the man whom it liberates.

To give oneself, to risk one's life, to be loyal, these are the actions that have made for grandeur in man. If you are searching for a model, you will find him in the pilot who gives his life to deliver his mail sack, in the doctor who dies on the front line of an epidemic, or in the meharist who leads his Moorish platoon deeper and deeper into solitude and privation.

Their sacrifice may seem to you futile, but do you really believe that they have not served? They have impressed a fine image upon the fresh clay of humanity, they have sowed fertile seed in the mind of the child who is lulled to sleep by stories born of their deeds. Nothing is lost; the wall-girt monastery glows with light.

Somewhere along the way we have made a wrong turn. Oh

yes, the human anthill is richer than ever; we have at our disposal more material goods and greater leisure, yet we lack some essential thing that we cannot exactly define. As human beings we feel diminished; we have lost some of man's mysterious prerogatives.

At Juby, I raised gazelles. Down there everyone raised gazelles. We kept them in an airy trellised shelter, for gazelles must have free-flowing air. No creature in the world is more fragile than they, yet if they are captured young they do survive. They learn to eat out of your hand, they allow you to stroke them, they nuzzle your cupped palm with their soft, moist noses. And you, you imagine that you have tamed them. You have protected them, you think, against the obscure chagrin that noiselessly snuffs out a gazelle's life, bringing it the most gentle of deaths.

Then one day you find them standing with their little horns lowered, pushing against the wall of their enclosure in the direction of the desert. It is as if they have been riveted by some magnet. They do not know they are fleeing from you. They come to drink the milk you have brought them, they allow you to stroke them, they thrust their noses even more softly into the cup of your hand. But you have scarcely turned away when, after the semblance of a lighthearted gallop, they are drawn back to the trellised wall. If you do not intervene, they will remain there. They do not try to buck the wall; they simply drop their heads and stand with their little horns pressing against it until they die.

What is it? The mating season? Or simply their hunger for

a fine, breathless gallop? The creatures do not know. Their eyes were not even open when you captured them. They have never known the freedom of the sands or the scent of the male. But you are more intelligent than they. You know what it is they thirst for—it is space, space in which they can achieve their true nature. They want to become gazelles, to dance their dance. They want to know that arrowing flight— two hundred miles an hour—broken by sudden leaps, as if tiny flames were spurting up here and there from the sand. What do jackals matter if for gazelles truth is the taste of jackal fear that makes them leap higher and run more fleetly? What does the lion matter if for gazelles truth is the flank laid open by one rip of the claw under the blazing sun? You look at their drooping heads and you think, It's nostalgia. Nostalgia, the desire for something, one knows not what. The object of desire exists, but the words to express it do not.

And we, what is it that we lack? What vista, what expanse are we asking be opened to us? We are struggling to escape, but the walls of our prison are thickening around us. Once upon a time, it was held that a proper upbringing required simply that we be fed, clothed, and all our material needs be taken care of. By this method little by little there was created a race of petty shopkeepers, small-time politicians, and technicians oblivious to any inner life. "But," you will remind me, "we are better educated, better informed than ever before. We benefit from all the manifold conquests of the human mind."

Anyone who supposes that the cultivation of the mind is

based on learning formulas and memorizing established solutions has a meager notion of the truly cultivated man. The lowliest graduate of the Polytechnique knows far more about Nature and Nature's laws than did Descartes, Pascal, or Newton. He is nonetheless incapable of a single soaring flight of intelligence such as these men knew. They were not "brought up"; they were cultivated. Pascal is, above all else, a style. Newton, above all, a man. He became the mirror of the universe. The ripe apple that fell to the ground, the stars in the July sky—he heard them, and they spoke the same language. For him, science was life.

We are amazed to discover what mysterious conditions are required to nourish the human spirit. We ourselves cannot draw a free breath unless we are bound to others by a common and disinterested ideal. We are the children of the age of comfort, yet we are filled with an inexpressible happiness when we share our last crust with others in the desert. To those of us who have known the joy of rescuing a crew downed in the Sahara, all other pleasures seem empty.

Let us, then, refrain from astonishment at what men do. One man finds that his essential manhood comes alive at the sight of self-sacrifice, cooperative effort, a rigorous vision of justice, manifested in an anarchist's cellar in Barcelona. For that man there will henceforth be but one truth—the truth of the anarchists. Another, having once mounted guard over a flock of terrified little nuns kneeling in a Spanish nunnery, will thereafter know a different truth—that it is sweet to die for the church.

154

What all of us want is to be set free. The man who sinks his pickax into the ground wants that stroke to mean something. The convict's stroke is not the same as the prospector's, for the obvious reason that the prospector's stroke has meaning and the convict's stroke has none. It would be a mistake to think that the prison exists at the point where the convict's stroke is dealt. Prison is not a mere physical horror. It is using a pickax to no purpose that makes a prison; the horror resides in the failure to enlist all those who swing the pick in the community of mankind.

We all yearn to escape from prison.

There are two hundred million men in Europe whose existence has no meaning and who yearn to come alive. Industry has torn them from the idiom of their peasant lineage and has locked them up in those enormous ghettos that are like railway yards heaped with blackened trucks. Out of the depths of their slums these men yearn to be awakened. There are others, caught in the wheels of a thousand trades, who are forbidden to share in the joys known to a Mermoz, to a priest, to a man of science.

Men can, of course, be stirred into life by being dressed up in uniforms and made to blare out chants of war. It must be confessed that this is one way for men to break bread with comrades and to find what they are seeking, which is a sense of something universal, of self-fulfillment. But of this bread men die.

It is easy to dig up wooden idols and revive ancient and more or less workable myths like Pan-Germanism or the

Roman Empire. The Germans can intoxicate themselves with the intoxication of being Germans and compatriots of Beethoven. A stoker in the hold of a freighter can be made drunk with this drink. What is more difficult is to bring up a Beethoven out of the stokehold.

These demagogic idols are carnivorous idols. The man who dies to advance science or to heal the sick serves life by his very dying. It may be splendid to die for a greater Germany or Italy or Japan; however, then the adversary is not the stubborn equation or the cancer that resists the serum; the adversary is the man next door. One must stand up to him, yes, but it can no longer be a question of vanquishing him. Today each side takes shelter behind a concrete wall and night after night sends out its squadrons that will drop the bombs that will blow the guts out of the other. Victory belongs to him who rots last—witness Spain—but in truth both rot together.

What had we to do in order to be born into life? Give ourselves. We have sensed dimly that man can commune with man only in terms of a shared image. Pilots meet if they are fighting to deliver the same mail; the Brown Shirts, if they are offering their lives to the same Hitler; the mountain climbers, if they are aiming for the same peak. Men do not unite by moving toward each other directly but only by losing themselves in the same god.

In a world become a desert we thirst for comradeship. It is the savor of bread broken with comrades that makes us accept the values of war. But there are other ways than war to bring us the warmth of a race, shoulder to shoulder, toward an identical goal. War has tricked us. It is not true that hatred adds anything to the exaltation of the race.

We will win our way through to freedom if we can help each other recognize a common aim that unites all men, rather than to look for abstract solutions. The surgeon does not listen to the patient's complaining as he checks his pulse but perceives the whole man whom he hopes to cure; the surgeon speaks a universal language. The mail pilot needs a wrist of iron to keep his plane clear of the backwash, and it is a cruelly grueling job. But as he fights to hold his course, he also serves human relations. The power in his hand and wrist links people who, in their mutual love, are trying to keep in touch; the pilot, too, shares in the universal. And the simple shepherd who watches over his flock under the stars, were he to become aware of his role, would discover that he is more than a shepherd. He is a sentinel. And each sentinel stands guard over the whole of the empire.

Why cheat the stoker by setting him, in the name of Beethoven, against his neighbor? What wicked hypocrisy that is, when the same country throws Beethoven into a concentration camp if he does not think like the stoker. The stoker must aim to grow, and one day speak, like Beethoven, a universal language.

If we reach out for this awareness of the Universe, we will once more find the true path of man. The tradesmen who have tranquilly set up shop by the river's edge but do not see the current flowing by are not the only ones who are oblivious

157

of it. Yet the world does evolve. From molten lava and star dust life is born. Slowly, slowly we have pulled ourselves up until we can write cantatas and weigh nebulae. The political agent, with the shells bursting above his head, knows that the genesis is not complete and that he must pursue his way upward. Life moves on toward a larger awareness. Slowly, slowly, the star dust composes and nourishes its finest flower.

The shepherd who discovers that he is a sentinel has already attained his full stature.

When we shall be moving forward in the right direction—the path we set out upon when we awoke from the primeval slime—then and then only will we be happy. Then we shall be able to live in peace, for that which gives meaning to life gives meaning to death.

Death is sweet when it comes in its time and in its place, when it is part of the order of things, when the old peasant of Provence, at the end of his reign, remits into the hands of his sons his parcel of goats and olive trees in order that they in their turn may transmit them to their sons. When one is part of a peasant lineage, one's death is only half a death. Each life in turn bursts like a pod and sends forth its seed.

I stood once with three peasants in the presence of their dead mother. Sorrow filled the room. For a second time, the umbilical cord had been cut. For a second time the knot had been loosed, the knot that bound one generation to another. Of a sudden the three sons had felt themselves alone on earth with everything still to be learned. The magnetic pole round which they had lived was gone; their mother's table, where they had collected on feast days with their families, was no more. But I could see in this rupture that it was possible for life to be granted a second time. Each of these sons was now to be the head of a family, was to be a rallying point and a patriarch, until that day when each would pass on the staff of office to the brood of children now murmuring in the court-yard.

I looked at their mother, at the old peasant with the firm peaceful face, the tight lips, the human face transformed into a stone mask. I saw in it the faces of her sons. That mask had served to mold theirs. That body had served to mold the bodies of these three exemplary men who stood there as up-right as trees. And now she lay broken but at rest, a vein from which the gold had been extracted. In their turn, her sons and daughters would bring forth men from their mold. One does not die on a farm. Their mother is dead, long live their mother!

Sorrowful, yes, but so simple was this image of a lineage dropping one by one its white-haired members as it made its way through time and through its metamorphoses toward a truth that was its own.

VII.

MEN AND
MACHINES

This preface was written for a special issue of *Documents*, August 1, 1939, which was devoted to test pilots.

Jean-Marie Conty will be speaking to you about test pilots. Now, Conty is a Polytechnique man. He believes in equations, and he is right. The equation is to the experiment as the bottle is to the wine. Yet in fact a new machine is rarely born of mathematical analysis the way the chick is hatched from the egg. Mathematical analysis may precede the experiment but often merely codifies it—which, after all, is a necessary function, too. Rough experiments, let's say, indicate that in a given phenomenon variations are accurately represented by such and such a hyperbolic curve. The experimenter uses the equation for the hyperbola to codify his initial measurements. By painstaking analysis, he also demonstrates that his results could not have been otherwise. Further and more controlled experiments enable him to refine his curve—which now begins to look more and more like the curve of an altogether different formula. He uses a new equation to codify his new measurements with even more scrupulous care. He will also demonstrate, just as meticulously as before, how these new results had all been foreseeable from the beginning of time.

The theorist believes in logic. He believes, also, that he despises Dreams and Intuition and Poetry. He does not see that these three fairies have donned disguises to seduce him, as if he were some simple schoolboy. He does not realize that he owes his finest discoveries to them. They appear before him in the guise of Working Hypotheses and Absolute Constants and Analogies. So how could he suspect that when he heeded them, he was betraying his austere logic and was listening to the Muses sing?

Jean-Marie Conty will tell you about the wonderful life of the test pilot. But he is a Polytechnique man, and he will assure you that presently the test pilot will be nothing but a measuring rod for the engineer. Of course, I believe this, too. I also believe that the day is coming when, if we don't know what ails us, we will put ourselves in the hands of doctors who will waste no time asking us questions; they will take a syringeful of blood, and from that sample they will deduce various constants that they will then multiply one by the other, after which, having consulted various logarithmic tables, they will prescribe the pill that will make us well.

However, when I feel sick I intend to go to Doctor Y. Doctor Y will be an elderly country doctor. He will study me out of the corner of his eye, tap my belly, spread a snowy old handkerchief across my shoulders and lean his ear against it to listen. Then he will give a little cough, light his pipe, stroke his chin—and as the first step in helping me get well, he will smile at me.

I still believe in men to whom the airplane means more than a collection of parameters, for whom it is an organism whose breathing and heartbeat they listen to. They bring the plane down. They walk quietly around it. With the tip of their fingers, they stroke the fuselage, tap a wing. They are not calculating; they are meditating. Then they turn to the mechanic and say simply, "There you are. . . . Stabilizer needs to be shortened a bit."

I admire Science, of course. But I also admire Wisdom.

VIII.

A FERTILE
ANGUISH

This preface appeared in the French translation of Anne Morrow Lindbergh's *Listen! the Wind*, published by Corrêa, Paris, in 1939.

As I was reading this book, I was reminded of what a friend of mine said once about some war reportage by an American newspaperman that he found excellent. "Here is one reporter," he said, "who's had the good taste simply to report. He got his stories first-hand and he doesn't interlard them with comment. And he doesn't fictionalize, either. Sometimes he simply quotes a ship's log. He's so right to stay in the background, for what emerges from that kind of stark testimony —from just the raw document—is remarkable poetry and pathos. Why do people hanker to embellish reality? It's stupid. Reality is beautiful in itself. Suppose those sailors decide someday to write about their war experiences. They will sweat over bad novels or bad poems, and be utterly unaware that the raw material they have at hand is pure gold."

I don't agree with this. Maybe those sailors will write bad poems, but the same men would have kept dull diaries, too. The problem has to do not with the evidence but with the witness. The point is not the adventure but the adventurer. Reality cannot be directly rendered. Reality is a pile of bricks that can assume many forms. Even if the journalist did write his book in telegraphic style, even if he crammed it full of concrete detail, he nonetheless interposed himself between reality and the expression he gave to it. He chose his material—surely he did not relate everything?—and he imposed a certain order upon it. *His* order. By imposing his order upon the raw material at hand, he built his own building.

What is true of concrete facts is also true of words. Now, I'm going to throw out a few words at random—*cours* (courtyard), *pavé* (pavement), *bois* (wood), *retentir* (echo). You demur. These are not words, you contend, that arouse an emotional response. However, put such verbal raw material into the hands of Baudelaire, and he will show you that from these neutral words he can construct a great image:

"Le bois retentissant sur le pavé des cours. . . ."

Words like "courtyard" or "wood" or "pavement" can be made to move the heart as well as words like "autumn" or "moonlight." What is more, I see no reason why the author who works with underwater pressures, gyroscopes, and sight lines cannot engage our emotions with such material as well as he can with memories of love. Where I really part company with my friend is that I fail to see why this same author could not engage us with memories of love as easily as with his gyroscopes, sight lines, and underwater pressures. I have flipped through many books that were so much sentimental guff. I have also read articles by the dozen that aspired to stir me to the core of my being with accounts of how the needle on the pressure gauge dropped. The needle is falling; the hero's life is in danger; his survival is obviously linked to the fate of the anxious wife who waits for him—but if the author happens to have no talent, I can't care less. Facts in and by themselves are not moving. The death of the hero is sad indeed, especially if he leaves an unconsolable wife behind, but no author can contrive to stir our feelings twice as deeply by making his hero a bigamist.

Obviously, the crux of the problem lies in the relationship between reality and writing, or, rather, between reality and thought. How does one convey emotion? What has one actually conveyed by expressing oneself? What is the essence?

The essence, I believe, is as distinct from the materials utilized as the nave of a cathedral is different from the heap of stones from which it emerged. What one can attempt to seize, translate, and transmit—whether from the external or inner world—is relationships. "Structures," as the doctors put it. Think for a moment of a metaphor. Its value resides on a plane other than that of the words actually used. It does not reside in any one of the elements one is associating but in the kind of liaison that is specified—in a particular inner attitude that the word structure imposes. The image is an action that binds the reader unbeknownst to him; the reader is not moved, he is cast under a spell.

This is why Anne Lindbergh's book seems to me something quite different from a forthright account of her flying adventures. This is why it is beautiful. Now, it is true that in her book the author has mustered only concrete facts, technical observations and reflections—in a word, the raw materials of her profession. But this is not the point. What could it matter to me to learn that this takeoff was difficult or that that wait-over was long, or that in the course of the flight Anne Lindbergh was bored or in high spirits. All this is only the *gangue*. The question is: What did she extract from it? What face did she put on these experiences? Is the essence of a work of art created as the structure is built that will capture it? No. The snare and the thing snared are not of the same essence. Consider the builder of cathedrals. He has used stones, and out of stones he has built silence.

A true book is like a net, and words are the mesh. The nature of the mesh matters relatively little. What matters is the live catch the fisherman draws up from the depths of the sea, the flashings of silver that we see gleam within the net. What has Anne Lindbergh brought back from her inner universe? What is the flavor of her book?

This is difficult to say, for to convey its flavor one must write and speak of many things. Nevertheless . . . I sense a faint anguish suffusing these pages. It takes different forms, but it circulates tirelessly through the book like a silent blood stream.

It is my observation that every profoundly coherent creative work can almost always be reduced to an elementary common denominator. I remember a film in which, without the director's being aware of it, the real hero was heaviness. Everything in this film weighed heavily. Atavism weighed upon a degenerate emperor; heavy winter furs weighed on his shoulders; crushing responsibilities weighed on his prime minister. Even the doors in the film were heavy. And in the last scene you saw the conqueror, burdened by his heavy victory, slowly climb a shadowy stairway toward the light. Now, this common denominator of heaviness was not a preconceived effect. The author had not planned it. But the fact that it was there and could be detected was the sign of the film's subterranean continuity.

I remember also the gist, not the exact words, of a strange remark Flaubert made about his *Madame Bovary:* "I was trying, first of all, to express the particular shade of yellow you find in the crack of a wall where cockroaches hatch."

Reduced thus to a rudimentary formula, what Anne Lindbergh has expressed is an unease that is caused by a tendency to be late. How hard it is to move forward in step with an inner rhythm when one must struggle against the inertia of the physical world. Everything is always so nearly on the verge of grinding to a halt. One must be most vigilant if one is to preserve life and motion in a universe that is threatening to break down. . . .

Lindbergh is out in a small boat in a Porto Praia bay, checking water currents. From the crest of a hill, his wife watches him labor like a tiny insect mired in a huge, sticky trap. She walks on, and every time she turns to the sea, it seems to her that her husband has made no headway. The insect flutters its wings in vain. How difficult to cross a bay; if one were to slow down just a little, one would never reach the sea. . . .

For several days they have been prisoners of this island where time has no meaning, where time does not move. Here men live and die in the same place; in a whole lifetime they will have conceived one idea, only one and always the same, until the day comes when even that simply stops.

"I am *chef* here," their host tells them a dozen times over, until the repetition becomes as meaningless as a distant echo. But for them time must be set in motion again. They must rejoin the continent, reenter the stream, return to where men are worked hard, where they can change and be alive. Anne Lindbergh is afraid not of death but of eternity.

Eternity is so near! It is so easy never to cross the bay, never to escape from an island, never to get the plane off the ground at Bathurst. They are both, she and Lindbergh, a little late. . . . Only a little late. . . . Hardly late at all. . . . But let the delay be one moment too long, and no one in the world waits for you.

We have all known the little girl who can't run as fast as the others. The others are playing up ahead. "Wait for me! Wait for me!" But she has fallen behind, and they are going to get tired of waiting and they are going to leave her behind, forget her, and she will be all alone in the world. How should one reassure her? This kind of anguish is incurable. For if she takes part in their game now, and then has to leave, and is slow about leaving, she will wear out their patience. They're murmuring among themselves already, they're already looking at her askance. . . . They are going to leave her alone again, all alone.

It is an extraordinary revelation to see this kind of inner anxiety in a couple whom the whole world has applauded. When a telegram from Bathurst informs them that they are welcome to land there, lo and behold, they are infinitely grateful. Later, at Bathurst, they are unable to take off as planned, and they are embarrassed by what seems to them an imposition. It is not a question of false modesty on their part; it is their sense of mortal danger. A small delay, and everything is lost.

Such anguish is fertile. It is this inner compunction—and nothing will ever cure it—that makes them start out two hours before dawn, outpioneer even the pioneers, cross oceans that hold other men in check.

This is a far cry from the fast-paced action of the stereotyped adventure story. In her book, Anne Lindbergh is secretly leaning on something as impossible to formulate, as elemental and universal as a myth. Yet, through all the technical data and observations, she is able to make us acutely aware of the problem of the human condition. She is not writing *about* the airplane but *via* the airplane. Her professional imagery serves as her vehicle for conveying to us something at once concealed and essential.

Lindbergh has not been able to get his plane airborne at Bathurst. It is overloaded. For such a pilot, however, a sea breeze would be enough to enable him to take off. But the wind has fallen. Once again, the travelers struggle vainly in the sticky trap. Then they decide to sacrifice: the less essential food, accessories, and spare parts are jettisoned. Again and again they attempt a takeoff, and each time they fail they decide on fresh sacrifices. Little by little, the floor of their room is littered with precious objects that they weigh out ounce by ounce and regretfully cast aside.

The professional setback is actually relatively minor, yet Anne Lindbergh expresses it with gripping veracity. Furthermore, she never mistakes the pathos of the airplane. This is not found in sun-gilded clouds at sunset. Sun-gilded clouds are rubbish. It is to be found in the use of a screwdriver—when, for example, you are working on an empty socket that gapes like a broken tooth among the orderly array of dials on an instrument panel. Make no mistake, however. Mrs. Lindbergh has been able to make the lay reader as well as the working pilot share their dejection because she has moved beyond a purely professional disappointment to a more general pathos. She has rediscovered the old myth of sacrifice whereby salvation is achieved. We were already familiar with other forms of it—the trees that must be pruned if they are to bear fruit; the men who within the prison walls of a monastery discover the full breadth of the spirit and who pass from renunciation to renunciation until they achieve plenitude.

But the help of the gods is needed, too. Anne Lindbergh has rediscovered Fatality. To prune the heart of man is not enough to save him; he must also be touched by grace. To prune the tree is not enough for it to bud; spring must also have a hand in the matter. To lighten the load is not enough for the plane to take off; a gust of wind from the sea is needed.

Quite effortlessly, Anne Lindbergh has restored Iphigenia to life. She writes on a sufficiently high level for her struggle against time to assume the significance of a struggle against death, for the lack of a breeze at Bathurst to confront us almost imperceptibly with the problem of destiny—and to make us feel how the hydroplane, which on the water is nothing but a heavy, cumbersome machine, changes substance and becomes a pure, pulsing blood stream when the grace of the sea wind has touched it.

IX.

THE PILOT AND
THE ELEMENTS

Saint-Exupéry was assigned the responsibility of plotting the last section of Areopostal Argentina's air routes, from Comodoro Rivadavia to Punta Arenas. He flew the reconnaissance missions himself and established the bases at Comodoro Rivadavia–San Julián, and Punta Arenas, and organized the two at Trelew and Bahia Blanca. After inspecting the airport installations at Pacheco, Saint-Exupéry took off in a Laté-26 on his first exploratory flight in the extreme south.

Saint-Exupéry's account of his battle with the cyclone that was raging over Patagonia from Cape Horn toward the Strait of Magellan has been compared to Conrad's *Typhoon*.

It appeared in the weekly *Marianne*, No. 356, on August 16, 1939.

When Joseph Conrad described a typhoon he said very little about towering waves, or darkness, or the whistling of the wind in the shrouds. He knew better. Instead, he took his reader down into the hold of the vessel, packed with emigrant coolies, where the rolling and the pitching of the ship had ripped up and scattered their bags and bundles, burst open their boxes, and flung their humble belongings into a crazy heap. Family treasures painfully collected in a lifetime of poverty, pitiful mementoes so alike that nobody but their owners could have told them apart, had lost their identity and lapsed into chaos, into anonymity, into an amorphous magma. It was this human drama that Conrad described when he painted a typhoon.

Every airline pilot has flown through tornados, has returned out of them to the fold—to the little restaurant in Toulouse where we sit in peace under the watchful eye of the waitress—and there, recognizing his powerlessness to convey what he has been through, has given up the idea of describing hell. His descriptions, his gestures, his big words would have made the rest of us smile as if we were listening to a little boy bragging. And necessarily so. The cyclone of which I am about to speak was, physically, much the most brutal and overwhelming experience I ever underwent; and yet beyond a certain point I do not know how to convey its violence except by piling one adjective on another, so that in the end I should convey no impression at all—unless that of an embarrassing taste for exaggeration.

It took me some time to grasp the fundamental reason for this powerlessness, which is simply that I should be trying to describe a catastrophe that never took place. The reason why writers fail when they attempt to evoke horror is that horror is something invented after the fact, when one is re-creating the experience over again in memory. Horror does not manifest itself in the world of reality. And so, in beginning my story of a revolt of the elements which I myself lived through I have no feeling that I shall write something which you will find dramatic.

I had taken off from the field at Trelew and was flying down to Comodoro Rivadavia, in the Patagonian Argentine. Here the crust of the earth is as dented as an old boiler. The high-pressure regions over the Pacific send the winds past a gap in the Andes into a corridor fifty miles wide through which they rush to the Atlantic in a strangled and accelerated buffeting that scrapes the surface of everything in their path. The sole vegetation visible in this barren landscape is a planta-tion of oil derricks looking like the after-effects of a forest fire. Towering over the round hills on which the winds have left a residue of stony gravel, there rises a chain of prow-shaped, saw-toothed, razor-edged mountains stripped by the elements down to the bare rock.

For three months of the year the speed of these winds at ground level is up to a hundred miles an hour. We who flew the route knew that once we had crossed the marshes of Trelew and had reached the threshold of the zone they swept, we should recognize the winds from afar by a gray-blue tint in the atmosphere at the sight of which we would tighten our belts and shoulder straps in preparation for what was coming. From then on we had an hour of stiff fighting and of stumbling again and again into invisible ditches of air. This was manual labor, and our muscles felt it pretty much as if we had been carrying a longshoreman's load. But it lasted only an hour. Our machines stood up under it. We had no fear of wings suddenly dropping off. Visibility was generally good, and not a problem. This section of the line was a stint, yes. It was certainly not a drama.

But on this particular day I did not like the color of the sky.

The sky was blue. Pure blue. Too pure. A hard blue sky that shone over the scraped and barren world while the fleshless vertebrae of the mountain chain flashed in the sunlight. Not a cloud. The blue sky glittered like a new-honed knife. I felt in advance the vague distaste that accompanies the prospect of physical exertion. The purity of the sky upset me. Give me a good black storm in which the enemy is plainly visible. I can measure its extent and prepare myself for its attack. I can get my hands on my adversary. But when you are flying very high in clear weather the shock of a blue storm is as disturbing as if something collapsed that had been holding up your ship in the air. It is the only time when a pilot feels that there is a gulf beneath his ship.

Another thing bothered me. I could see on a level with the mountain peaks not a haze, not a mist, not a sandy fog, but a sort of ash-colored streamer in the sky. I did not like the look of that scarf of filings scraped off the surface of the earth and borne out to sea by the wind. I tightened my leather harness as far as it would go and I steered the ship with one hand while with the other I hung on to the longeron that ran alongside my seat. I was still flying in remarkably calm air.

Very soon came a slight tremor. As every pilot knows, there are secret little quiverings that foretell your real storm. No rolling, no pitching. No swing to speak of. The flight continues horizontal and rectilinear. But you have felt a warning drum on the wings of your plane, little intermittent rappings scarcely audible and infinitely brief, little cracklings from time to time as if there were traces of gunpowder in the air.

And then everything round me blew up.

Concerning the next couple of minutes I have nothing to say. All that I can find in my memory is a few rudimentary notions, fragments of thoughts, direct observations. I cannot compose them into a dramatic recital because there was no drama. The best I can do is to line them up in a kind of chronological order.

In the first place, I was standing still. Having banked right in order to correct a sudden drift, I saw the landscape freeze abruptly where it was and remain jiggling on the same spot. I was making no headway. My wings had ceased to nibble into the outline of the earth. I could see the earth buckle, pivot— but it stayed put. The plane was skidding as if on a toothless cogwheel.

Meanwhile I had the absurd feeling that I had exposed myself completely to the enemy. All those peaks, those crests, those teeth that were cutting into the wind and unleashing its gusts in my direction, seemed to me so many guns pointed straight at my defenseless person. I was slow to think, but the thought did come to me that I ought to give up altitude and make for one of the neighboring valleys where I might take shelter against a mountainside. As a matter of fact, whether I liked it or not I was being helplessly sucked down toward the earth.

Trapped this way in the first breaking waves of a cyclone about which I learned, twenty minutes later, that at sea level it was blowing at the fantastic rate of one hundred and fifty miles an hour, I certainly had no impression of tragedy. Now, as I write, if I shut my eyes, if I forget the plane and the flight and try to express the plain truth about what was happening to me, I find that I felt weighed down, I felt like a porter carrying a slippery load, grabbing one object in a jerky movement that sent another slithering down, so that, overcome by exasperation, the porter is tempted to let the whole load drop. There is a kind of law of the shortest distance to the image, a

psychological law by which the event to which one is sub-
jected is visualized in a symbol that represents its swiftest
summing up: I was a man who, carrying a pile of plates, had
slipped on a wax floor and let his scaffolding of porcelain
crash.

I found myself imprisoned in a valley. My discomfort was
not less, it was greater. I grant you that a down current has
never killed anybody, that the expression "flattened out by a
down current" belongs to journalism and not to the language
of fliers. How could air possibly pierce the ground? But here
I was in a valley at the wheel of a ship that was three-quarters
out of my control. Ahead of me a rocky prow swung to left
and right, rose suddenly high in the air for a second like a
wave over my head, and then plunged down below my horizon.

Horizon. There was no longer a horizon. I was in the wings
of a theater cluttered up with bits of scenery. Vertical,
oblique, horizontal, all of plane geometry was awhirl. A hundred transversal valleys were muddled in a jumble of perspec-
tives. Whenever I seemed about to take my bearings a new
eruption would swing me round in a circle or send me tumbling wing over wing and I would have to try all over again
to get clear of all this rubbish. Two ideas came into my mind.
One was a discovery: for the first time I understood the cause
of certain accidents in the mountains when no fog was present
to explain them. For a single second, in a waltzing landscape
like this, the flyer had been unable to distinguish between

vertical mountainsides and horizontal planes. The other idea was a fixation: The sea is flat; I shall not hook anything out at sea.

I banked—or should I use that word to indicate a vague and stubborn jockeying through the east-west valleys? Still nothing pathetic to report. I was wrestling with chaos, was wearing myself out in a battle with chaos, struggling to keep in the air a gigantic house of cards that kept collapsing despite all I could do. Scarcely the faintest twinge of fear went through me when one of the walls of my prison rose suddenly like a tidal wave over my head. My heart scarcely skipped a beat when I was tripped up by one of the whirling eddies of air that the sharp ridge darted into my ship. If I felt anything unmistakably in the haze of confused feelings and notions that came over me each time one of these powder magazines blew up, it was a feeling of respect. I respected that sharp-toothed ridge. I respected that peak. I respected that dome. I respected that transversal valley opening out into my valley and about to toss me God knew how violently as soon as its torrent of wind flowed into the one on which I was being borne along.

What I was struggling against, I discovered, was not the wind but the ridge itself, the crest, the rocky peak. Despite my distance from it, it was the wall of rock I was fighting with. By some trick of invisible prolongation, by the play of a secret set of muscles, this was what was pummeling me. It was against this that I was butting my head. Before me on the right I recognized the peak of Salamanca, a perfect cone which, I knew, dominated the sea. It cheered me to think I was about to escape out to sea. But first I should have to wrestle with the gale off that peak, try to avoid its down-crushing blow. The peak of Salamanca was a giant. I was filled with respect for the peak of Salamanca.

There had been granted me one second of respite. Two seconds. Something was collecting itself into a knot, coiling itself up, growing taut. I sat amazed. I opened astonished eyes. My whole plane seemed to be shivering, spreading outward, swelling up. Horizontal and stationary it was, yet lifted before I knew it fifteen hundred feet straight into the air in a kind of apotheosis. I who for forty minutes had not been able to climb higher than two hundred feet off the ground was suddenly able to look down on the enemy. The plane quivered as if in boiling water. I could see the wide waters of the ocean. The valley opened out into this ocean, this salvation. —And at that very moment, without any warning whatever, half a mile from Salamanca, I was suddenly struck straight in the midriff by the gale off that peak and sent hurtling out to sea.

There I was, throttle wide open, facing the coast. At right angles to the coast and facing it. A lot had happened in a single minute. In the first place, I had not flown out to sea. I had been spat out to sea by a monstrous cough, vomited out of my valley as from the mouth of a howitzer. When, what seemed to me instantly, I banked in order to put myself where I wanted to be in respect of the coastline, I saw that the coastline was a mere blur, a characterless strip of blue; and I was five miles out to sea. The mountain range stood up like a crenelated fortress against the pure sky while the cyclone crushed me down to the surface of the waters. How hard that wind was blowing I found out as soon as I tried to climb, as soon as I became conscious of my disastrous mistake: throttle wide open, engines running at my maximum, which was one hundred and fifty miles an hour, my plane hanging sixty feet over the water, I was unable to budge. When a wind like this one attacks a tropical forest it swirls through the branches like a flame, twists them into corkscrews, and uproots giant trees as if they were radishes. Here, bounding off the mountain range, it was leveling out the sea.

Hanging on with all the power in my engines, face to the coast, face to that wind where each gap in the teeth of the range sent forth a stream of air like a long reptile, I felt as if I were clinging to the tip of a monstrous whip that was cracking over the sea.

In this latitude the South American continent is narrow and the Andes are not far from the Atlantic. I was struggling not merely against the whirling winds that blew off the east-coast range, but more likely also against a whole sky blown down upon me off the peaks of the Andean chain. For the first time in four years of airline flying I began to worry about the strength of my wings. Also, I was fearful of bumping the sea—not because of the down currents which, at sea level, would necessarily provide me with a horizontal air mattress, but because of the helplessly acrobatic positions in which this wind was buffeting me. Each time that I was tossed I became afraid that I might be unable to straighten out. Besides, there was a chance that I should find myself out of fuel and simply drown. I kept expecting the gasoline pumps to stop priming, and indeed the plane was so violently shaken up that in the half-filled tanks as well as in the gas lines the gasoline was sloshing round, not coming through, and the engines, instead of their steady roar, were sputtering in a sort of dot-and-dash series of uncertain growls.

I hung on, meanwhile, to the controls of my heavy transport plane, my attention monopolized by the physical struggle and my mind occupied by the very simplest thoughts. I was feeling practically nothing as I stared down at the imprint made by the wind on the sea. I saw a series of great white puddles, each perhaps eight hundred yards in extent. They were running toward me at a speed of one hundred and fifty miles an hour where the down-surging windspouts broke against the surface of the sea in a succession of horizontal explosions. The sea was white and it was green— white with the whiteness of crushed sugar and green in puddles the color of emeralds. In this tumult one wave was indistinguishable from another. Torrents of air were pouring down upon the sea. The winds were sweeping past in giant gusts as when, before the autumn harvests, they blow a great flowing change of color over a wheatfield. Now and again the water went incongruously transparent between the white pools, and I could see a green and black sea-bottom. And then the great glass of the sea would be shattered anew into a thousand glittering fragments.

It seemed hopeless. In twenty minutes of struggle I had not moved forward a hundred yards. What was more, with flying as hard as it was out here five miles from the coast, I wondered how I could possibly buck the winds along the shore, assuming I was able to fight my way in. I was a perfect target for the enemy there on shore. Fear, however, was out of the question. I was incapable of thinking. I was emptied of everything except the vision of a very simple act. I must straighten out. Straighten out. Straighten out.

There were moments of respite, nevertheless. I dare say those moments themselves were equal to the worst storms I had hitherto met, but by comparison with the cyclone they were moments of relaxation. The urgency of fighting off the wind was not quite so great. And I could tell when these intervals were coming. It was not I who moved toward those zones of relative calm, those almost green oases clearly painted on the sea, but they that flowed toward me. I could read clearly in the waters the advertisement of a habitable province. And with each interval of repose the power to feel and to think was restored to me. Then, in those moments, I began to feel I was doomed. Then was the time that little by little I began to tremble for myself. So much so that each time I saw the unfurling of a new wave of the white offensive I was seized by a brief spasm of panic which lasted until the exact instant when, on the edge of that bubbling cauldron, I bumped into the invisible wall of wind. That restored me to numbness again.

Up! I wanted to be higher up. The next time I saw one of those green zones of calm it seemed to me deeper than before and I began to be hopeful of getting out. If I could climb high enough, I thought, I would find other currents in which I could make some headway. I took advantage of the truce to essay a swift climb. It was hard. The enemy had not weakened. Three hundred feet. Six hundred feet. If I could get up to three thousand feet I was safe, I said to myself. But there on the horizon I saw again that white pack unleashed in my direction. I gave it up. I did not want them at my throat again; I did not want to be caught off balance. But it was too late. The first blow sent me rolling over and over and the sky became a slippery dome on which I could not find a footing.

One has a pair of hands and they obey. How are one's orders transmitted to one's hands?

I had made a discovery that horrified me: my hands were numb. My hands were dead. They sent me no message. Probably they had been numb a long time and I had not noticed it. The pity was that I had noticed it, had raised the question. That was serious.

Lashed by the wind, the wings of the plane had been dragging and jerking at the cables by which they were controlled from the wheel, and the wheel in my hands had not ceased jerking a single second. I had been gripping the wheel with all my might for forty minutes, fearful lest the strain snap the cables. So desperate had been my grip that now I could not feel my hands.

What a discovery! My hands were not my own. I looked at them and decided to lift a finger. It obeyed me. I looked away and issued the same order. Now I could not feel whether the finger had obeyed or not. No message had reached me. I thought, "Suppose my hands were to open; how would I know it?" I swung my head round and looked again. My hands were still locked round the wheel. Nevertheless, I was afraid. How can a man tell the difference between the sight of a hand opening and the decision to open that hand, when there is no longer an exchange of sensations between the hand and the brain? How can one tell the difference between an image and an act of the will? Better stop thinking of the picture of open hands. Hands live a life of their own. Better not offer them this monstrous temptation. And I began to chant a silly litany which went on uninterruptedly until this flight was over. A single thought. A single image. A single phrase tirelessly chanted over and over again: "I shut my hands. I shut my hands. I shut my hands." All of me was condensed into that phrase and for me the white sea, the whirling eddies, the saw-toothed range ceased to exist. There was only "I shut my hands." There was no danger, no cyclone, no land unattained. Somewhere there was a pair of rubber hands which, once they let go the wheel, could not possibly come alive in time to recover from the tumbling drop into the sea.

I had no thoughts. I had no feelings except the feeling of being emptied out. My strength was draining out of me and so was my impulse to go on fighting. The engines continued their dot-and-dash sputterings, their little crashing noises that were like the intermittent cracklings of a ripping canvas. Whenever they were silent longer than a second I felt as if a heart had stopped beating. There! That's the end. No, they've started up again.

The thermometer on the wing, I happened to see, stood at twenty below zero, but I was bathed in sweat from head to foot. My face was running with perspiration. What a dance! Later I was to discover that my storage batteries had been jerked out of their steel flanges and hurtled up through the roof of the plane. I did not know then, either, that the ribs on my wings had come unglued and that certain of my steel cables had been sawed down to the last thread. And I continued to feel strength and will oozing out of me. Any minute now I should be overcome by the indifference born of utter weariness and by the mortal yearning to take my rest.

What can I say about this? Nothing. My shoulders ached. Very painfully. As if I had been carrying too many sacks too heavy for me. I leaned forward. Through a green transparency I saw sea-bottom so close that I could make out all the details. Then the wind's hand brushed the picture away.

In an hour and twenty minutes I had succeeded in climbing to nine hundred feet. A little to the south—that is, on my left—I could see a long trail on the surface of the sea, a sort of blue stream. I decided to let myself drift as far down as that stream. Here where I was, facing west, I was as good as motionless, unable either to advance or retreat. If I could reach that blue pathway, which must be lying in the shelter of something not the cyclone, I might be able to move in slowly to the coast. So I let myself drift to the left. I had the feeling, meanwhile, that the wind's violence had perhaps slackened.

It took me an hour to cover the five miles to shore. There in the shelter of a long cliff I was able to finish my journey south. Thereafter I succeeded in keeping enough altitude to fly inland to the field that was my destination. I was able to stay up at nine hundred feet. It was very stormy, but nothing like the cyclone I had come out of. That was over.

On the ground I saw a platoon of soldiers. They had been sent down to watch for me. I landed nearby and we were a whole hour getting the plane into the hangar. I climbed out of the cockpit and walked off. There was nothing to say. I was very sleepy. I kept moving my fingers, but they stayed numb. I could not collect my thoughts enough to decide whether or not I had been afraid. Had I been afraid? I couldn't say. I had witnessed a strange sight. What strange sight? I couldn't say. The sky was blue and the sea was white. I felt I ought to tell someone about it since I was back from so far away! But I had no grip on what I had been through. "Imagine a very white sea . . . very white . . . whiter still." You cannot convey things to people by piling up adjectives, by stammering.

195

You cannot convey anything because there is nothing to convey. My shoulders were aching. My insides felt as if they had been crushed in by a terrible weight. You cannot make drama out of that, or out of the cone-shaped peak of Salamanca. That peak was charged like a powder magazine; but if I said so, people would laugh. I would myself. I respected the peak of Salamanca. That is my story. And it is not a story.

There is nothing dramatic in the world, nothing pathetic, except in human relations. The day after I landed I might get emotional, might dress up my adventure by imagining that I who was alive and walking on earth was living through the hell of a cyclone. But that would be cheating, for the man who fought tooth and nail against that cyclone had nothing in common with the fortunate man alive the next day. He was far too busy.

I came away with very little booty indeed, with no more than this meager discovery, this contribution: How can one tell an act of the will from a simple image when there is no transmission of the senses?

I could perhaps succeed in upsetting you if I told you some story of a child unjustly punished. As it is, I have involved you in a cyclone, probably without upsetting you in the least. This is no novel experience for any of us. Every week men sit comfortably at the cinema and look on at the bombardment of some Shanghai or other, some Guernica, and marvel without a trace of horror at the long fringes of ash and soot that twist their slow way into the sky from those man-made volcanoes. Yet we all know that together with the grain in the granaries, with the heritage of generations of men, with the treasures of families, it is the burning flesh of children and their elders that, dissipated in smoke, is slowly fertilizing those black cumuli.

The physical drama itself cannot touch us until someone points out its spiritual sense.

X.

AN OPEN LETTER
TO FRENCHMEN
EVERYWHERE

Following the British-American landings in North Africa and the German occupation of southern France, Saint-Exupéry published a long article in Montreal's *Canada* on November 30, 1942, that dealt with the urgency for Frenchmen everywhere to unite. Translated into English, the article had appeared the day before in the *New York Times Magazine*. This hastily written appeal was broadcast over all French-language programs of the Office of War Information and republished in North African newspapers.

First of all, France! The German night has swallowed up the country. For a time we were still able to know a little about those we love; we could still send them words of affection, even if we could not share the wretched bread on their tables. From afar we could catch their breathing.

All that is over now. France is nothing but a silence; she is lost somewhere in the night with all lights out, like a ship. Her mind and spirit have been absorbed into her physical being. We shall not know even the names of the hostages who to-morrow will die before the German rifles.

It is always in the cellars under a tyranny that new truths are born. Let us not play the part of braggarts. There are forty million people over there in France who must endure their slavery. We shall not be carrying any fire of the spirit to those who are already nourishing the flame with their life's blood—like the wax of a candle. They will deal with French problems better than we can; they have all the right to deal with them. Our talk about sociology, politics, and art will carry no weight with them. They will not read our books, they will not listen to our speeches. Perhaps our ideas may make them sick.

Let us be infinitely modest. Our political discussions are the discussions of ghosts; ambitions among us are comic. We do not represent France; all we can do is to serve her. And whatever we do, we shall have no just claim for recognition. For there is no common measure between freedom to fight and bearing the crushing weight of the darkness. There is no common measure between the métier of the soldier and the métier of the hostage. The people over there in France are the only true saints. Even if we have the honor of taking part in the battle, we shall still be in their debt. There, in the first place, is the fundamental truth.

Men of France, let us be reconciled in order to serve!

I shall say a few words about the quarrels which have divided Frenchmen in the hope of doing something to remove them. For there has been a grave spiritual disorder among French people. The souls of many among us have been torn; these have need of peace of mind, and they should find it. By the miracle of American action in North Africa, all our different roads have led us to the same meetingplace. Why now should we get bogged down in the old quarrels? It is time to unite, not to divide, for opening wide the arms, not for exclusions.

Were our quarrels worth the hate we wasted on them? Who can ever maintain that he alone is absolutely right? Man's field of vision is minute; language is an imperfect instrument; the problems of life burst all the formulas.

We were all in agreement as to our faith. We all wanted to save France. France had to be saved both in flesh and in the spirit. Of what use is the spiritual heritage if there be no heir? What good is the heir if the spirit be dead?

All of us hate the idea of collaboration. Some of us accused France of real collaboration while others saw only a ruse. Let us think of Vichy as a trustee in bankruptcy, negotiating with a greedy conquerer for delivery to France of a little grease for railroad cars. (France can no longer get gasoline, or even horses, to bring food to her towns.) The officers of the Armistice Commission will one day tell us about this persistent and atrocious German blackmail. A quarter-turn of the key—delivery of any less grease than required—and a hundred thousand more French children would die in the next six months.

When a single hostage is shot, his sacrifice shines forth. His death is the cement that binds French unity. But when the Germans, by merely holding up an agreement on grease for cars, kill a hundred thousand hostages of five years, where is the compensation for this slow, silent hemorrhage? What is the acceptable fixed price for dead children? What would have been the tolerable limit of Vichy's concession in its attempt to save them? Who can say?

You are aware that French denunciation of the armistice terms would have been equivalent to a return to a state of war. It would have justified the conqueror's seizure of all adult males as military prisoners. This blackmail lay heavily over France. The threat was plainly set forth. German blackmail is no jest. The rot of German prison camps yields only corpses. My country was thus threatened, purely and simply, with utter extermination, under legal and administrative pretense, of six million men. France was armed only with sticks to resist this slave hunt. Who is in a position to say for certain what should have been her resistance?

Here at last is the seizure of North Africa by the Allies within sixty-six hours to prove, perhaps, that in spite of blackmail and in spite of two years of pressure, Germany has failed seriously to encroach upon this North African territory. Somewhere, then, there must have been attempts at resistance. Perhaps the victory in North Africa has been won, at least in part, by our five hundred thousand children who have died. Who would dare say that the number is insufficient?

Frenchmen, if we could reduce our differences of opinion to their true proportions, that would be enough to make peace among us. We have never been divided except on the question as to the weight to be attributed to the Nazi blackmail. On the one hand, some said, "If the Germans are determined to wipe out the people of France, they will wipe them out, whatever the French do. This blackmail ought to be despised. Nothing should make Vichy take such and such a decision or give this or that promise."

On the other hand, other people thought: "It is not merely a case of blackmail but of blackmail unique for cruelty in the history of the world. Let France, refusing all capital concessions, employ every sort of ruse to delay the menace from day to day. The tone of the official utterances shows that when a Ulysses or Talleyrand is disarmed, there remain to him only words with which to deceive the enemy."

Do you believe, Frenchmen, that these diverse opinions as to the rigors of the Nazi blackmail or as to the real intentions of this circumscribed government really ought to make us hate one another still? (When the English and the Russians fight side by side, they leave to the future disputes which are grave enough.) Our divergences of opinion do not touch our hatred of the invader, while at the same time we are all indignant, as are all the people of France, at the surrender of the foreign refugees, a violation of the right of asylum.

Well, these quarrels of the past have no longer any point. Vichy is dead. Vichy has carried with it to the grave all its inextricable problems, its contradictory personnel, its sincerity, its ruses, its cowardice, and its courage. Let us leave for the time being the role of judge to the historians and the courts-martial after the war. It is more important to serve France in the present than to argue about her history.

The German occupation of all France has settled all our quarrels and brought appeasement to the drama of our consciences. Men of France, are you willing to become reconciled? There is no longer even a shadow of a reason for argument among us. Let us abandon all party spirit. Why should we hate one another? Why should we be jealous of one another? There is no question of positions to be won. There is no question of any race for offices. The only places open are soldiers' places—perhaps some quiet beds in some little cemetery in North Africa.

The military law of France binds all men up to forty-eight. From eighteen to forty-eight we ought all of us to be mobilized. There is no question whether we wish to enlist or not. It is demanded of us, in order to turn the balance of war, that we take our places in the scale—altogether and quite simply.

Although our old quarrels are now merely quarrels for the historians, there is another danger of disunion among us. Let us have the courage, men of France, to surmount this danger.

Some among us trouble themselves about the name of one leader as against another, of one form of government as against another. They see the phantom of injustice rising on the horizon.

Why do they thus complicate matters? There is no injustice to fear. None of our personal interests is going to suffer in the future. When a mason devotes himself to the building of a cathedral, the cathedral cannot injure the mason. The only role expected of us is a war role. I myself feel wonderfully safe against any form of injustice. Who could do me an injustice since I have only one idea—namely, to rejoin in Tunis my comrades of Group 2/33 with whom I lived through nine months of the campaign and then the brutal German offensive, which took two-thirds of our number, and finally the escape to North Africa on the eve of the armistice? Let us not dispute now about precedence, about honors, about justice, or about priorities. There is nothing of all that offered to us. They are only offering us rifles—and there will be plenty of these for everybody.

If I feel so much at peace now it is because again I find in myself no leaning toward the position of a judge. The group of which I become a part is neither a party nor a sect, it is my country. I am not interested in who will command us. The provisional organization of France is an affair of state. Let us leave it to Britain and to the United States to do the best they can. If our ambition is to press the trigger of a machine gun we shall not be worried about decisions that will seem to us secondary. Our real chief is France, now condemned to silence. Let us hate parties, clans, divisions of any kind.

If the only desire we formulate (and we have the right to formulate it, since it unites all of us) is to obey the military leaders rather than the political leaders, it is like the military salute which honors not the soldier who is saluted but the nation which he represents. We know what General de Gaulle and General Giraud think about authority. They serve. They are the first servants. That should be enough for us, since all the quarrels which weakened us yesterday are now resolved or absorbed in the present.

Here, it seems to me, we stand. Our friends in the United States should not get a false picture of France. Some regard Frenchmen as a little like a basket of crabs. This is unjust. Only the controversialists talk. One does not hear those who keep still.

I suggest to all those Frenchmen who have up to this time been silent that they emerge from their silence just once to reassure Cordell Hull as to the true state of our spirit. I suggest that each of these send to him some such telegram as the following:

We ask the privilege of serving in any way whatever. We desire the mobilization of all Frenchmen in the United States. We accept in advance any organization that may be deemed the most desirable. But, hating any spirit of division among Frenchmen, we ask simply that the organization be outside politics.

The state department will be astonished at the number of Frenchmen who will take their stand for unity. For, despite our reputation, most of us at heart know only love of our civilization and our country.

Frenchmen, let us become reconciled! When we find ourselves one day together in a bomber fighting five or six Messerschmitts, the thought of our old fights will make us smile.

During the war, in 1940, when I came back from a mission with my plane shot full of holes, I used to drink an excellent Pernod at the squadron bar. I often won my Pernod throwing dice, sometimes from a Royalist comrade, perhaps from one who was a Socialist, or perhaps from Lieutenant Israel, the bravest of our crew, who was a Jew. And we all clinked glasses in the greatest friendliness.

XI.

LETTER TO
GENERAL X

Early in 1943, Group 2/33, the air-combat unit to which Saint-Exupéry had belonged until the fall of France, was re-forming in North Africa under Allied command, and he was determined to rejoin it. Passage was difficult to obtain because of his civilian status, but he pulled every available string and finally managed to be shipped out with a United States convoy, reaching Algiers on May 4, 1943.

Saint-Exupéry was first assigned to the French squadron stationed at a desert depot two hundred miles south of Algiers, where the pilots had only old Bloch machines for training. Another squadron, based in Oudjda, near the Algerian-Moroccan frontier, was working with P-38s. (This, the Lockheed Lightning, was the fastest and most advanced plane then in combat service.) The preferred age for a P-38 pilot was twenty to twenty-five; the maximum age allowable was thirty-five. Saint-Exupéry was forty-three and in poor health. Nonetheless, he was able to wangle a transfer and authorization to fly a limited number of reconnaissance missions over France.

The "Letter to General X" was written during the early days of his training with the P-38. It reflects the intense nervous strain under which he was living and working, and a deeper depression as well. Some two months afterward, he left on the mission from which he did not return. The manuscript was found among his papers and published much later, in *Le Figaro Littéraire* of April 10, 1948.

By now I have flown the P-38 several times. It is a fine plane. I should have been very happy to have such a gift when I was twenty. But I must regretfully say that today, at forty-three and after sixty-five hundred hours of flying time, it provides a kind of sport I no longer relish. The plane has become a mere transportation device—and, in this instance, a war machine. If I submit to the speed and altitude it exacts, at what in this profession is a patriarchal age, it is not because I hope to recapture the satisfactions of youth but because I refuse not to down my share of the bilge my generation must swallow.

Maybe this is a sad commentary, maybe not. Very likely, I was wrong when I was twenty. In any event, I am reminded that three years ago, in October, 1940, I returned to France from North Africa, where Group 2/33 had emigrated. I found that my old car had been put up in some garage or other, and so it happened that I discovered the horse and trap. And through them, the green of our roadsides, and sheep, and olive trees. Olive trees began to play what was for me a new role. They were no longer metronomes that beat time as they flashed by at eighty miles an hour. Now they were revealed in their true rhythm, which is the rhythm of the slow production of olives. Sheep were no longer a factor in depressing the day's average on the stock exchange. Sheep became living creatures again. They dropped real dung, they grew real wool. Grass acquired meaning, too, since sheep cropped it.

I felt then as if I were coming back to life in that one corner of the earth where even the dust is fragrant. (I'm being unfair. It is fragrant in Greece, too, and in Provence.) I felt as if all my life long I'd been an idiot.

I tell you all this by way of explaining to you how herdlike our existence is here in the heart of this American air base. We wolf our food, standing, in a matter of minutes; 2600-horsepower planes buzz incessantly overhead; we are boxed into sleeping cubicles, three to a cell—but what really matters is that we live in a frightful human desert. Nothing here lifts the heart. Back in 1940, we flew missions that we knew had no purpose and we ourselves had little hope of getting back; it was a kind of illness that had to be lived through, and so is this. I shall be "ill" in this sense for an undetermined period of time. I don't see that I have any right to refuse to endure the illness. That's all there is to it. But I am sad, sad to the depths of my being—not for myself but for my generation, which is so miserably impoverished. It is a generation that has known bars, calculating machines, and Bugattis exclusively as the forms of spiritual life, and now it finds itself caught up in herdlike action that has lost all human meaningfulness.

Think what war meant only a hundred years ago. It fused a complex of efforts that harmonzied with some part of man's spiritual or poetic nature, or responded at least to some needs of human existence. Today we are as dehydrated as bricks. We smile at such foolishness as flags, songs, music, victories. Indeed, today there is no such thing as victory, nothing that offers the poetic density of an Austerlitz. Today we have the phenomena of the slow or fast digestion. All that other was so much nonsense, not only foolish but false. As a consequence, now men refuse to be roused to any kind of spiritual life whatever. They dutifully carry out their assembly-line tasks. As the young Americans put it: "It's a thankless job. Do it and get it over with." (The psychological warfare experts the world over must be cudgeling their brains in despair.)

What afflicts young people is not any lack of capacity, however; it's that they are forbidden, on pain of appearing old-fashioned, to draw strength from the great restoring myths of mankind. Ours is a decadent society that has declined from the level of Greek tragedy to the clichés of escapist comedy. (How much lower can one sink?) Ours is the age of publicity and the point system, of totalitarian governments and armies without flags or bugles or services for their dead. . . . I hate my own period with all my heart. Today man is dying of thirst.

There is only one problem, General, only one problem in the whole world. It is the need to restore a spiritual meaning to men's lives, and to reawaken their capacity for spiritual disquiet. Were I a believer, once this "thankless job" was finished, I would listen to nothing but Gregorian chants. All men need such a rain to rain down upon them. It is impossible to survive on refrigerators, politics, balance sheets, and cross-word puzzles, you see! It is impossible! It is impossible to live without poetry and color and love.

Listen to any folk song of the fifteenth century, and you can measure how far we have fallen. Nothing remains but the voice of the propaganda machine. (You must forgive me.) Two million men hear nothing but the robot, they under-stand nothing but the robot, they themselves are becoming robots. All the creaking disorders of the last thirty years had their origin in two things: problems created by a nineteenth-century economic system, and spiritual despair. Why did a man like my friend Mermoz follow that great booby of a fascist colonel if not from thirst? Why Russia? Why Spain? Men have tested Cartesian values and found that except in the field of the natural sciences they turn out rather poorly. Now there is only one problem, only one: we must rediscover the fact that there is a life of the spirit even more noble than the life of the mind, and that it alone can nourish mankind.

What I am saying spills over into the area of religion, but that is only one of the forms it may take. A spiritual life may lead one ultimately to some religion, but it begins when a human being is conceived as an entity over and above his component parts. The love of home, for example—a love that is unknowable in the United States—belongs to the spiritual life.

So does a village festival. So does respect for the dead. I mention this because since I arrived here two or three para-chutists have been killed, and I have seen how quickly they

216

were whisked off the scene. They had served their purpose. Now, this behavior is not peculiar to Americans; it is characteristic of our period. Man no longer has meaning.

It is absolutely essential that we speak to men.

What good will it do to win this war if we then face a century-long crisis of revolutionary epilepsy? Once the question of German aggression is settled, the real problems will begin to emerge. It is quite unlikely that speculation on the New York Stock Exchange will suffice at the end of this war, as it did in 1919, to distract humanity from its real troubles. If a strong spiritual force is absent, there will be dozens of sectarian faiths sprouting up like so many mushrooms, each at odds with the other. A quaintly outdated Marxism will disintegrate into a swarm of competitive neo-Marxisms. (This is already evident in Spain.) Unless, of course, a French Caesar appears and installs us in a new-socialist concentration camp for all eternity. . . .

Ah, this is a strange evening in this strange, small world. I can see, from this room, the windows lighting up in faceless walls. I hear the radio stations grind out their canned music for an idle crew of men who have come from beyond the sea and do not even know what homesickness is.

One can mistake resigned acceptance for a spirit of sacrifice or moral stature. That would be a grave mistake, however. The bonds of love that attach the man of today to other human beings and to other things are so slack, so tenuous, that man no longer feels absence as he once did. I remember a terrible line from some Jewish joke: "So you're leaving? But you'll be so far away!" Away from where? The "where" that was being left was little more than a vast bundle of habits. For ours is a period of divorce. We divorce a person as readily as we throw away an object. Refrigerators can be replaced. So can a home when it is merely a collection of objects. And a wife, and a religion, and a political party. One cannot even be unfaithful. Unfaithful to whom? to what? . . . Far from where? Man lives in a desert.

And how well behaved and orderly these herd-men are! I keep thinking of how those old Breton sailors disembarked at Punta Arenas and of Foreign Legionnaires loosed on a town —those complex knots of violent appetite and unbearable homesickness that human males become when they are held in too tight check. Keeping such men in line called for strong police or strong principles or strong faith. Today, depending on the accident of birth, men are held in line by a game of *belote* or by a game of bridge. We are, quite simply, castrated. And therefore, in one sense we are free. Let's say that we have had our arms and legs lopped off and been set free to walk.

But I detest this period in which a universal totalitarianism has converted men into cattle—docile, passive, unprotesting cattle. This, they want us to believe, is moral progress! What I hate in Marxism is the totalitarianism it leads to. Man is defined as a producer and a consumer, and the basic problem is distribution. What I hate in Nazism is the totalitarianism inherent in its very nature. The workers of the Ruhr are marched past a Van Gogh, a Cézanne, and a cheap print.

218

Naturally, they vote for the print. This is the people's truth! The budding Cézannes and Van Goghs, all the great nonconformists, are solidly immured in concentration camps while the browbeaten herd is fed cheap prints. Where is America heading, where are we all heading in this reign of universal bureaucracy? The robot man, the ant man, scurries from assembly line to card table. He is castrated, drained of all creative potency; even in his own village he can no longer make up a dance or a song for himself, because he is fed a ready-made, standardized culture the way steers are fed hay. This is the man of today.

I sometimes think how it was possible, not three hundred years ago, to write a book like *La Princesse de Clèves*, in which, because a woman has lost a passionate love, she shuts herself away in a convent for life. Of course, people kill themselves today. But the agony these people feel is on the order of a violent toothache. It may be unbearable, but it has nothing to do with love.

First things must come first, I agree. The war must be fought and won. I cannot bear the idea that generations of French children should be poured into the maw of the German Moloch. Our national substance is threatened. But when that will have been made secure, we will face the problem that is fundamental in our time: What is the meaning of man? To this question no answer is being offered, and I have the feeling that we are moving toward the darkest era our world has ever known.

It does not matter to me that I may be killed in this war. Of all that I have loved, what will remain? I am speaking not only of people but of customs, of irreplaceable modulations, of a certain spiritual light, of lunch under the olive trees on a farm in Provence, of Handel. The things that will survive I don't give a damn about!

What does matter is a certain ordering of things. Civilization is an intangible possession; it does not reside in things but in the invisible bonds that link them one to the other in this way and not in that way. Suppose we do achieve the mass distribution of perfectly machined musical instruments; where will the musician be?

The possibility that I may be killed in this war is not important. It is not important that I fly into a rage over these new airborne torpedos. (It is nonetheless true that they have nothing to do with planes or with flying and that they transform a pilot, all hemmed around by push buttons and dials, into a kind of head bookkeeper. Flying is also a matter of a certain ordering of connections.) But if I do come back alive from the thankless job that must be done, it will be to face only one challenge: What can one, what must one, say to men?

I am less and less sure why I am writing you all this. Probably in order to say it to someone, since I have no right to write about such things. We must not disturb people's peace of mind, we must not muddy the issues. No. For the moment, the best we can do is to turn into head bookkeepers and stick to our warplanes.

Since I began to write you, my two companions here in the

room have fallen asleep. I shall have to go to bed, too, for I suppose my light disturbs them. (How I miss a corner to myself!) In their way, they are marvelous comrades. Upright, generous, decent, loyal. Still, when I see them asleep like this, I don't know why but I feel a kind of impotent pity. If they are unaware of their own anxiety, I feel it. Upright, generous, decent, loyal—yes, but so terribly poor. They so badly need a God.

Forgive me if this dim flashlight that I will now snap off has kept you from sleeping, too, and believe me. . . .

Your friend . . .

AN EPILOGUE: AN APPEAL FOR PEACE

On April 22, 1945, the New York *Times* ran the following news item:

Charles Boyer, screen star and French patriot, yesterday made a plea over the Columbia Broadcasting System network for Franco-American fraternity by reading part of an essay written by his countryman, Antoine de Saint-Exupéry, French aviator and novelist, just before taking off on a flight in the present war from which he never returned. The part read by Mr. Boyer follows:

My American Friends: I would like to do you full justice. One day perhaps more or less serious differences will arise between us. All nations are selfish. All nations consider their selfishness sacred. It may be that your consciousness of your material power will one day cause you to take advantages which seem unfair to us. It may be that there will arise one day between us more or less serious arguments. If war is always won by believers, the peace treaties are sometimes dictated by businessmen.

But even if one day in my heart I form reproaches against the decisions of these men, these reproaches will never make me forget the nobility of the war aims of your people. To the quality of your deepest feelings I shall always pay the same tribute.

Look, my American friends, it seems to me that something new is in formation on our planet. The material progress of modern times has indeed linked mankind by a sort of nervous system. The contacts are innumerable. The communications are instantaneous. We are materially bound like the cells of the same body. But this body does not yet have a soul. This organism has not yet grown conscious of itself. The hand does not feel itself a part with the eye.

Your young men are dying in a war which for the first time in the history of the world is for them, in spite of all its honors, a confused experience of love. Do not betray them! Let it be they who dictate their peace when the day comes! May this peace resemble them! This war is noble. Let their faith in progress ennoble also the peace.

INDEX

Index

229

Index

ABOUT THE AUTHOR

The turn of the nineteenth century marked the advent of the airplane and the birth of French novelist, essayist, and aviator, Antoine de Saint-Exupéry. By the 1940's aviation had become the science of the day, and Saint-Exupéry its most articulate spokesman.

The pioneer pilot took his first monoplane ride at the age of eleven and wrote his first poem at seven. His life thereafter was dedicated to his twin loves—aviation and belles lettres. In 1931, Saint-Exupéry was awarded the Prix Femina for his novel *Night Flight*, and in 1939 his *Wind, Sand and Stars* received the Grand Prix of the French Academy and the acclamation of the world. In the midst of his literary achievements, Saint-Exupéry flew the first French airmail service over South America, Africa, and Indochina; he copiloted the French flying-boat *Lieutenant de Vaisseau Paris* on its first trip from France to the United States; he served as an air reconnaissance officer in World War II. At the fall of France he made his way to the United States, where he lived until American landings in North Africa enabled him to return to flying dangerous air missions for France—and to an untimely death. In July of 1944 the world mourned the news that Saint-Exupéry, the poet of the air age, had disappeared while in flight over the Mediterranean.

It is fitting that this last collection of Antoine de Saint-Exupéry's essays should be so representative of the man and the writer.